Bless This Child

Bless This Child

A Treasury of Poems, Quotations and Readings to Celebrate Birth

COLLECTED BY EDWARD SEARL

Skinner House Books
Boston

ISBN 1-55896-489-4
ISBN 978-1-55896-489-1

Printed in the United States
Cover art *Starry Messenger,* © 2002 Eleanor Rubin, http://ellyrubinjournal.typepad.com
Cover design by Kathryn Sky-Peck
Text design by Dartmouth Publishing, Inc.

09 08 07 06 05
6 5 4 3 2 1

We gratefully acknowledge permission to reprint copyrighted materials starting on page 157.

Library of Congress Cataloging-in-Publication Data

Bless this child : a treasury of poems, quotations, and readings to celebrate birth / collected by Edward Searl.
       p. cm.
    Includes index.
    ISBN 1-55896-489-4 (alk. paper)
  .1. Childbirth--Religious aspects--Meditations. 2. Child rearing--Religious aspects--Meditations. I. Searl, Edward, 1947-

BL625.8.B54 2005
808.8'03523--dc22

2005021733

Contents

Dear Reader,

A child comes into our world already formed and unique, an individual with an innate personality and latent abilities. This new child carries our collective hope for something more than the mere continuity of life.

Inevitably, we hope that the light that burns in us will burn more brightly in our children. We hope that each child will contribute to the progress of society, and in turn, that our society will be worthy of its children. We hope that each child will be personally fulfilled throughout the unfolding life that lies ahead.

This treasury of prose, poems, blessings, and readings gives voice to the many hopes and wishes that accompany the arrival of a new child. Culled from antiquity and from our contemporary world, written and spoken by parents, priests, and poets—the famous and the unknown—these passages are meant to inspire, to caution, and to shore us up for the great responsibility we have to care for and nurture all children.

There is no more inspiring aspect of the human condition than children, to whom this little book is dedicated.

Wishing you hope and joy,

Edward Searl

Full of Wonder

A child's world is fresh and new and beautiful, full of wonder and excitement. It is our misfortune that for most of us that clear-eyed vision, that true instinct for what is beautiful and awe-inspiring, is dimmed and even lost before we reach adulthood.

RACHEL CARSON

There was a child went forth every day;
And the first object he look'd upon, that object he became;
And that object became part of him for the day, or a certain part of
    the day, or for many years,
    or stretching cycles of years.

The early lilacs became part of this child,
And grass, and white and red morning-glories, and white and red
    clover, and the song of the phoebe-bird,
And the Third-month lambs, and the sow's pink-faint litter, and the
    mare's foal, and the cow's calf,
And the noisy brood of the barn-yard, or by the mire of the
    pond-side,
And the fish suspending themselves so curiously below there—
    and the beautiful curious liquid,
And the water-plants with their graceful flat heads—all became part
    of him.

WALT WHITMAN

The birth of a child, any child, is a new incarnation and carries the promise of the great miracle of humanity becoming divine, or reaching out to the stars.

DONALD B. KING

Ah, happy he who owns that tenderest joy,
The heart-love of a child.

LEWIS CARROLL

Our birth is but a sleep and a forgetting:
The Soul that rises with us, our life's Star,
Hath had elsewhere its setting,
And cometh from afar:
Not in entire forgetfulness,
And not in utter nakedness,
But trailing clouds of glory do we come
From God, who is our home:
Heaven lies about us in our infancy!

WILLIAM WORDSWORTH

Know you what it is to be a child?

It is to be something very different from the man of today. It is to have a spirit yet streaming from the waters of baptism; it is to believe in love, to believe in loveliness, to believe in belief; it is to be so little that the elves can reach to whisper in your ear;

it is to turn pumpkins into coaches, and mice into horses, lowness into loftiness, and nothing into everything, for each child has its fairy godmother in its own soul;

it is to live in a nutshell and to count yourself the king of infinite space . . . it is to know not as yet that you are under sentence of life, nor petition that it be commuted into death.

When we become conscious in dreaming that we dream, the dream is on the point of breaking; when we become conscious in living that we live, the ill dream is but just beginning.

FRANCIS THOMPSON

In countless upward-striving waves
The moon-drawn tide-wave strives;
In thousand far-transplanted grafts
The parent fruit survives;
So, in the new-born millions,
The perfect Adam lives.
Not less are summer-mornings dear

To every child they wake,
And each with novel life his sphere
Fills for his proper sake.

RALPH WALDO EMERSON

Comparisons

Child, when they say that others
 Have been or are like you,
Babes fit to be your brothers,
 Sweet human drops of dew,
Bright fruit of mortal mothers,
 What should one say or do?

We know the thought is treason,
 We feel the dream absurd;
A claim rebuked of reason,
 That withers at a word:
For never shone the season
 That bore so blithe a bird.

Some smiles may seem as merry,
 Some glances gleam as wise,
From lips as like a cherry
 And scarce less gracious eyes;

Eyes browner than a berry,
  Lips red as morning's rise.

But never yet rang laughter
  So sweet in gladdened ears
Through wall and floor and rafter
  As all this household hears
And rings response thereafter
  Till cloudiest weather clears.

When those your chosen of all men,
  Whose honey never cloys,
Two lights whose smiles enthrall men,
  Were called at your age boys,
Those mighty men, while small men,
  Could make no merrier noise.

Our Shakespeare, surely, daffed not
  More lightly pain aside
From radiant lips that quaffed not
  Of forethought's tragic tide:
Our Dickens, doubtless, laughed not
  More loud with life's first pride.

The dawn were not more cheerless
  With neither light nor dew

Than we without the fearless
     Clear laugh that thrills us through:
If ever child stood peerless,
     Love knows that child is you.

ALGERNON CHARLES SWINBURNE

When we behold a child, we behold the memory of generations etched in tiny features—noses, lips, eyes, chins, foreheads—distinctive characteristics that both make each child a unique individual and reflect a family heritage of ancestors near and far. When we behold a child, we behold the hope of a world yet to come. When we hold a child, we hold the hope of the world in our hands. Is this not holy?

DIANE DOWGIERT

Babyhood

A baby shines as bright
If winter or if May be
On eyes that keep in sight
A baby.

Though dark the skies or grey be,
It fills our eyes with light,
If midnight or midday be.

Love hails it, day and night,
The sweetest thing that may be
Yet cannot praise aright
A baby.

All heaven, in every baby born,
All absolute of earthly leaven,
Reveals itself, though man may scorn
All heaven.

Yet man might feel all sin forgiven,
All grief appeased, all pain outworn,
By this one revelation given.

Soul, now forget thy burdens borne:
Heart, be thy joys now seven times seven:
Love shows in light more bright than morn
All heaven.

What likeness may define, and stray not
From truth's exactest way,
A baby's beauty? Love can say not
What likeness may.

The Mayflower loveliest held in May
Of all that shine and stay not
Laughs not in rosier disarray.

Sleek satin, swansdown, buds that play not
As yet with winds that play,
Would fain be matched with this, and may not:
What likeness may?

Rose, round whose bed
Dawn's cloudlets close,
Earth's brightest-bred
Rose!

No song, love knows,
May praise the head
Your curtain shows.

Ere sleep has fled,
The whole child glows
One sweet live red
Rose.

ALGERNON CHARLES SWINBURNE

Behold the child, the visitor. He has come from nowhere, for he was not before this, and it is nowhere that he goes, wherefore he is called a visitor, for the visitor is one who comes from the unknown to stay but awhile and then to the unknown passes on again.

The child has come forth out of the great womb of the earth. The child has come forth to stand with star dust in his hair, with the rush of planets in his blood, his heart beating out the seasons of eternity, with a shining in his eyes like sunlight, with hands to shape with that same force that shaped him out of the raw stuff of the universe.

When one baby is born it is the symbol of all birth and life, and therefore all men must rejoice and smile, and all men must lose their hearts to a child.

KENNETH PATTON

He smiles, and sleeps!–sleep on,
And smile, thou little, young inheritor
Of a world scarce less young: sleep on and smile!
Thine are the hours and days when both are cheering
And innocent!

GEORGE GORDON LORD BYRON

Hold close one child, for his tiny bones carry the promise of all
   coming generations.
Live this moment in its fullness, for in it is all plenitude, all
   realization, all time.

KENNETH PATTON

I'm wandering around an outdoor fair and the light is starting to fade.
I've got my hot cup of glug in hand, and I'm feeling pretty toasty
despite the cold. Laura and Sophia are off looking at a booth some-
where. I hear Christmas music nearby, and eventually I find three
men playing "Silent Night," "We Wish You a Merry Christmas," and
other favorites. I stand there in the fading light and enjoy the smiles
of the people surrounding the musicians, their red cheeks, the holiday
cheer rising.

It's then that I notice the almost life-size manger scene near by. I wander over to it, not really expecting that it will be any different from any other manger scene I've ever run across. The critical voice in my head starts acting up. *It didn't really happen like that*, it says. *By the looks of the statues, you'd think that everyone involved in the gospel story was blond and blue-eyed.*

I almost turn away, but just then my eyes fall on Mary holding the baby Jesus tightly in her arms. All of a sudden I see it as if for the first time. The cynical voice in my head is gone. I finally see. The truly amazing thing here is not so much the birth of a great liberating prophet and spiritual leader—although that in itself is amazing and wonderful—but where and when it happens. It happens in the unlikeliest of places. It happens in a backwater town of Judea, in a dirty and rugged manger, in a time of crushing injustice and brutality and hopelessness. If Jesus can be born in a place and a time like this, what does that mean?

It means that Jesus can be born anywhere. Justice, compassion, and hope can be born anywhere. Even here and now.

ANTHONY DAVID

What is a Child? An experiment. A fresh attempt to produce the just man made perfect: that is, to make humanity divine.

GEORGE BERNARD SHAW

Nothing is strange to the child for whom everything is new.
Where all things are new nothing is novel.
The child does not yet know what belongs and what does not;
    therefore for him all things belong.
The ear of the child is open to all music.
His eyes are open to all arts.
His mind is open to all tongues.
His being is open to all manners.
In the child's country there are no foreigners.

KENNETH PATTON

Little children in particular are magic. They unite us all: parents and
non-parents, old and young, boys and girls, and women and men.
All are brought together by the arrival of a child. Infants are messengers from realms we do not remember. They also send back into the
universe the ongoing affirmation of life. A child is born and screams
at the indignity and the wonder of it all, and then, Scriabin writes,
"The universe resounds with the joyful cry I am."

LINDSAY BATES

What I see in little children is a fundamental freshness, a lack of knowledge about wickedness in the world. I see an urge toward life. That, as I see it, is the human vision of "The Kingdom of God." I believe that is why Jesus said to his disciples, "Suffer the little children to come unto me, for of such is the Kingdom of Heaven." Children come among us with unspoiled trust, with a potential for hope, with stars of expectation in their eyes, with a capacity for love and compassion.

THOMAS MIKELSON

In all their innocence, children offer us the treasure of their teachings. Although we think of ourselves as the teachers, driving home core values and imparting wisdom, in the presence of children we soon learn that we are the ones in training. Children reawaken us to the simple wonders of life. Looking at the morning dew, a spider's web, a tree in bud, a sunset, or the slow movement of a caterpillar through the eyes of a child is like seeing these things for the first time. Our task is to learn from the zest and wonder that all children bring into the world and that we too often lose in later life.

Children also enhance our humanity. As our interactions with children leave us less self-centered and more giving, loving, and patient, we have the opportunity to become more compassionate and caring human beings. And we learn about the really important things in life—like making angels in the snow.

Children encourage us to acknowledge other ways of seeing the world. They teach awareness, receptiveness, and the importance of keeping an open mind. It's hard to imagine the world from a child's point of view. And yet the ability to put aside our own reality and listen mindfully to what children are saying acknowledges their way of seeing the world and helps us in our own becoming.

CHERYL JACK

The child alone a poet is:
Spring and Fairyland are his.

ROBERT GRAVES

Children

Come to me, O ye children!
    For I hear you at your play,
And the questions that perplexed me
    Have vanished quite away.

Ye open the eastern windows,
    That look towards the sun,
Where thoughts are singing swallows
    And the brooks of morning run.

In your hearts are the birds and the sunshine,
    In your thoughts the brooklet's flow,
But in mine is the wind of Autumn
    And the first fall of the snow.

Ah! what would the world be to us
    If the children were no more?
We should dread the desert behind us
    Worse than the dark before.

What the leaves are to the forest,
    With light and air for food,
Ere their sweet and tender juices
    Have been hardened into wood,—

That to the world are children;
    Through them it feels the glow
Of a brighter and sunnier climate
    Than reaches the trunks below.

Come to me, O ye children!
    And whisper in my ear
What the birds and the winds are singing
    In your sunny atmosphere.

For what are all our contrivings,
    And the wisdom of our books,
When compared with your caresses,
    And the gladness of your looks?

Ye are better than all the ballads
    That ever were sung or said;
For ye are living poems,
    And all the rest are dead.

HENRY WADSWORTH LONGFELLOW

Thank God for little children,
Bright flowers by earth's wayside,
The dancing, joyous lifeboats
Upon life's stormy tide.

Thank God for little children;
When our skies are cold and gray,
They come as sunshine to our hearts,
And charm our cares away.

I almost think the angels,
Who tend life's garden fair,
Drop down the sweet wild blossoms
That bloom around us here.

It seems a breath of heaven
Round many a cradle lies,
And every little baby
Brings a message from the skies.

Frances Ellen Watkins Harper

Children remind us of the power of honesty and of the joy of being alive. And children, especially the youngest, have the natural ability to be totally present in any given moment. Free from anything like a list of *shoulds* or concerns about how they look or might sound, they can just *be*. This is what the Buddhists ask us to cultivate, in part, when they talk about cultivating the "beginner's mind." Children seem to live this kind of presence out naturally.

Just this weekend, all dressed up for a night out, I stepped into an elevator. At some point, I realized I was feeling a tug at my pants and looked down to see a little girl. Clearly she had seen my silk pants and wondered what they felt like, reached out to touch them, and liking what she felt, stood there rubbing the fabric between her fingers. All of us in the elevator had been lost in thought, thinking about our plans for the evening. She was living deeply in that moment, which just happened to involve my pants, until her mother saw and whisked the girl's hand away.

It isn't just Buddhism that exhorts us to imitate the beginner, the child. Christianity also often exhorts us to be like children. In fact, Jesus rebukes his disciples when they try to keep children out of his way, afraid they will be a nuisance: "Unless you become as little children, you shall not enter the kingdom of God." I read his words as a reminder to us all to recapture some of the simple trust and openness we had as children.

Children are the world's persistent plea for a renewal of hope and faith. The laughter of children recalls us so quickly to the beauty and the possibilities of this world. Enjoying a child's simple trust brings us back again and again to a willingness to trust others. Their delight in stories and their willingness to believe invites us to delight and to believe again too.

The stories of Judaism frequently include children bearing divine gifts, particularly wisdom. Young Joseph is given the gift of interpreting dreams and later leads a nation. Young Solomon asks for and receives the open heart that imparts wisdom and becomes the wisest man of his time. These stories remind the faithful that from the mouths of children and through their example, we can see evidence of some of the great religious truths. It is a lesson we would all be wise to keep in mind.

VANESSA RUSH SOUTHERN

La Befana arrives on January 6th, the same night that the three kings visited the baby Jesus. Like Santa, she is able to distribute toys to all the houses in a single night.

She is a very ancient and wise old spirit who knows something about the holy. She has an affinity for fire and chimneys, and in some places she arrives on a flying broom, though elsewhere she rides a donkey. In Italy, she has a connection with the ancestors and with the household gods of ancient days. Some families believe the gifts she delivers come from ancestors, representing the love and care of those who have gone before.

No, the child in your home may not be the one the Three Kings sought on their important, star-led mission. But la Befana knows that the child in your home is holy, worthy of gifts. Befana also knows that houses need to be cleaned. That God is in the details. If the house is clean, germs are kept at bay. If things are neat, there is less danger for little children. If everything has its place, it is easy to find what you need. The chickens have to be fed; the eggs must be gathered. The bills have to be paid, and things get out of hand if they aren't paid on time. The great kings and queens may have been able to go on a long journey to find one certain special baby, but someone else was keeping things in order for them at home.

There is always tension between going on that important journey, saying "yes" to following the star, and keeping the lawn mowed, the walk shoveled, the rent paid, and all the rest. The kings stand for saying "yes" to the big journey, to the important destination. La Befana stands for saying "no." Both have value.

Sometimes it's better to stay home. What we find by staying home is different. We visit not the one special baby, but the many, many other special babies.

MARY WELLEMEYER

Give Us the Child

Give us the child who lives within—
—the child who trusts,
—the child who imagines,
—the child who sings,
—the child who receives without reservation,
—the child who gives without judgment.

Give us a child's eyes, that we may receive the beauty and freshness of this day like a sunrise;

Give us a child's ears, that we may hear the music of mythical times;

Give us a child's heart, that we may be filled with wonder and delight;

Give us a child's faith, that we may be cured of our cynicism;

Give us the spirit of the child, who is not afraid to need; who is not afraid to love.

Amen.

SARAH YORK

My heart leaps up when I behold
  A rainbow in the sky:
So was it when my life began;
  So is it now I am a man;
So be it when I shall grow old,
  Or let me die!
The child is father of the man;
And I could wish my days to be
Bound each to each by natural piety.

WILLIAM WORDSWORTH

A child is valuable and irreplaceable, someone we cannot afford to lose. The world has embraced the truth that childhood shapes the women and men we are today. Because of this realization and deeper understanding, we have the ability to put a stop to destructive generational patterns and raise our sons and daughters with respect, self-esteem, and true commitment to their lives.

In the Dagara tribe, we know we cannot have community without children, we cannot have children without community, and neither would exist without spirit. It is one complete circle, each element completing the whole. We welcome our children and in so doing we welcome spirit.

SOBONFU SOMÉ

The dreams that charm'd me when a child,
Still linger with me yet,
For there are scenes of faded years,
I never can forget;
And there are eyes still beaming,
And hearts with friendships teeming,
That yet can great me ever,
With favor's warm embrace
And smiles that time can never
Dissemble or efface.

SEPTIMUS WINNER

Kids:
They dance before they learn
there is anything that isn't music.

WILLIAM STAFFORD

Grown-ups never understand anything for themselves, and it is tiresome for children to be always and forever explaining things to them.

ANTOINE DE SAINT-ÉXUPÉRY

To speak truly, few adult persons can see nature. Most persons do not see the sun. At least they have a very superficial seeing. The sun illuminates only the eye of the man, but shines into the eye and the heart of the child. The lover of nature is he whose inward and outward senses are still truly adjusted to each other; who has retained the spirit of infancy even into the era of manhood.

RALPH WALDO EMERSON

Maybe we should develop a Crayola bomb as our next secret weapon. A happiness weapon. A beauty bomb. And every time a crisis developed, we would launch one. It would explode high in the air—explode softly—and send thousands, millions, of little parachutes into the air. Floating down to earth—boxes of Crayolas. And we wouldn't go cheap, either—not little boxes of eight. Boxes of sixty-four, with the sharpener built right in. With silver and gold and copper, magenta and peach and lime, amber and umber and all the rest. And people would smile and get a little funny look on their faces and cover the world with imagination.

ROBERT FULGHUM

Children are remarkable for their intelligence and ardor, for their curiosity, their intolerance of shams, the clarity and ruthlessness of their vision.

ALDOUS HUXLEY

No day can be so sacred but that the laugh of a little child will make it holier still.

ROBERT INGERSOLL

Children, who play life, discern its true law and relations more clearly than men, who fail to live it worthily, but who think that they are wiser by experience, that is, by failure.

HENRY DAVID THOREAU

As a child, one has that magical capacity to move among the many eras of the earth; to see the land as an animal does; to experience the sky from the perspective of a flower or a bee; to feel the earth quiver and breathe beneath us; to know a hundred different smells of mud and listen unselfconsciously to the soughing of the trees.

VALERIE ANDREWS

The child with his sweet pranks, the fool of his senses, commanded by every sight and sound, without any power to compare and rank his sensations, abandoned to a whistle or a painted chip, to a lead dragoon, or a gingerbread-dog, individualizing everything, generalizing nothing, delighted with every new thing, lies down at night over-powered by the fatigue, which this day of continual pretty madness has incurred. But Nature has answered her purpose with the curly, dimpled lunatic. She has tasked every faculty, and has secured the symmetrical growth of the bodily frame, by all these attitudes and exertions—an end of the first importance, which could not be trusted to any care less perfect than her own.

RALPH WALDO EMERSON

To rescue our children we will have to let them save us from the power we embody: we will have to trust the very difference that they forever personify. And we will have to allow them the choice, without fear of death: that they may come and do likewise or that they may come and that we will follow them, that a little child will lead us back to the child we will always be, vulnerable and wanting and hurting for love and for beauty.

JUNE JORDAN

I remember the gleams and glooms that dart
    Across the schoolboy's brain;
The song and the silence in the heart,
That in part are prophecies, and in part
    Are longings wild and vain.

And the voice of that fitful song
Sings on, and is never still:
'A boy's will is the wind's will,
And the thoughts of youth are long, long thoughts.'

HENRY WADSWORTH LONGFELLOW

Here Under My Heart

Here, under my heart
you'll keep
till it's time
for us to meet,
& we come apart
that we may come
together,
& you are born
remembering
the wavesound
of my blood,
the thunder of my heart,
& like your mother
always dreaming
of the sea.

ERICA MANN JONG

I heard once of a tribal people in East Africa, who count the birthday
of a child not as the day of birth but as the day on which the mother
first became aware of the baby—whether because she was already
pregnant or because she began to wish for a child. When this happened, the mother-to-be would spend time sitting alone and listening
within for the song of the child. And when she began to hear it, she
would sing it until she knew it well and then teach it to the father.

Both would sing it in the evening before sleep, and it would be taught to the midwives before labor, so that as the child was born, the first sound to greet it would be the singing of its own song.

What a lovely way to think about our children—each one with a primordial, unique song all his or her own. Our task is to listen so carefully, so attentively, that we hear and learn the song. That's the way we're called to listen to our children, to listen to their words and beyond their words, to the sadness or excitement of their voices, to the sudden long silence, to the look on their faces, to the struggle to bring to the surface something that can't quite be articulated.

KATHLEEN MCTIGUE

Brit Kedusha

Here is your first gift
(this blessing, this echo):
sound you'll answer to
turning, always, to see who spoke.
Here is your name,
which people we don't know
will call you years from now,
when your infant face
with its astonished look

is just a picture
and our huge, parental love
a blur of hands.

JODY BOLZ

Living with an infant is an intense retreat with the power of breaking down the ego, opening the heart to the way things actually are, allowing the whole self to be present for a mystery unfolding. And the mystery unfolds with lightning speed, leaving new parents with a sense that every moment is a bit of cosmic foam tossed up by the waves of the universe, to be taken in right now or lost forever. Some get into photos, others into stories, and still others into silent raptures. Parenting an infant can call us out of ourselves, into a different, more caring and connected way of being in the world.

This intense time yields gradually to another stage, when things can be more under control, and the question becomes: Will the insights remain? We met the highest teacher for a brief moment, but now here is this child we think we know, growing and changing at a more manageable pace. Does the heart stay open? Does the mind stay focused on what is truly present? Does the heart remember the sense that this is a mystery unfolding?

MARY WELLEMEYER

Dear Baby,

Do you know that today, two years ago, your Daddy and I met? It was on an inner tube race! Your Daddy wore orange shorts and blue shades. He still wears the same sunglasses and I'm sure that he'll be wearing the same ones until he's old and gray.

You know, your Mommy should be exercising. She has been so lazy since she found out about you. Tomorrow she'll start! I promise. All I want to do is sit and think about you, just like I did in the weeks after I met your Daddy. But I know that exercise will make us both happy.

Well, baby, its dinnertime, so I must feed us. Remember, I love you to pieces, so does your Daddy, and we can't wait to see you.

Love,
Mommy

KATHERINE SEARL BODNAR

A Shadow

I shall always remember one winter evening, a little before Christmastime, when I took a long, solitary walk in the outskirts of the town. The cold sunset had left a trail of orange light along the horizon, the dry snow tinkled beneath my feet, and the early stars had a keen, clear lustre that matched well with the sharp sound and the frosty sensation. For some time I had walked toward the gleam of a distant window, and as I approached, the light showed more and more clearly through the white curtains of a little cottage by the road. I stopped, on reaching it, to enjoy the suggestion of domestic cheerfulness in contrast with the dark outside. I could not see the inmates, nor they me; but something of human sympathy came from that steadfast ray.

As I looked, a film of shade kept appearing and disappearing with rhythmic regularity in a corner of the window, as if some one might be sitting in a low rocking-chair close by. Presently the motion ceased, and suddenly across the curtain came the shadow of a woman. She raised in her arms the shadow of a baby, and kissed it; then both disappeared, and I walked on.

What are Raphael's Madonnas but the shadow of a mother's love, so traced as to endure forever? In this picture of mine, the group actually moved upon the canvas. The curtains that hid it revealed it. The ecstasy of human love passed in brief, intangible panorama before me. It was something seen, yet unseen; airy, yet solid; a type, yet a reality; fugitive, yet destined to last in my memory while I live. It said more to me than would any Madonna of Raphael's, for his mother never kisses her child. I believe I have never passed over that road since then, never seen the house, never heard the names of its occupants. Their character, their history, their fate, are all unknown. But these two will always stand for me as disembodied types of humanity,—the Mother and the Child; they seem nearer to me than my immediate neighbors, yet they are as ideal and impersonal as the goddesses of Greece or as Plato's archetypal man.

THOMAS WENTWORTH HIGGINSON

I know a baby, such a baby—
Round blue eyes and cheeks of pink,
such an elbow furrowed with dimples,
such a wrist where creases sink.

"Cuddle and love me, cuddle and love me,"
crows the mouth of coral pink:
Oh, the bald head, and oh the sweet lips,
And, oh, the sleepy eyes that wink.

CHRISTINA ROSSETTI

Poppies

She loves blood-red poppies for a garden to walk in.
In a loose white gown she walks
   and a new child tugs at cords in her body.
Her head to the west at evening when the dew is creeping,
A shudder of gladness runs in her bones and torsal fiber:
She loves blood-red poppies for a garden to walk in.

CARL SANDBURG

The Salutation

These little Limbs,
These Eys and Hands which here I find,
This panting Heart wherwith my Life begins;
Where have ye been? Behind
What Curtain were ye from me hid so long!
Where was, in what Abyss, my new-made Tongue?

When silent I
So many thousand thousand Years
Beneath the Dust did in a Chaos ly,
How could I Smiles, or Tears,
Or Lips, or Hands, or Eys, or Ears perceiv?
Welcom ye Treasures which I now receiv.

I that so long
Was Nothing from Eternity,
Did little think such Joys as Ear and Tongue
To celebrat or see:
Such Sounds to hear, such Hands to feel, such Feet,
Beneath the Skies, on such a Ground to meet.

New burnisht Joys!
Which finest Gold and Pearl excell!
Such sacred Treasures are the Limbs of Boys

In which a Soul doth dwell:
Their organized Joints and azure Veins
More Wealth include than all the World contains.

From Dust I rise
And out of Nothing now awake;
These brighter Regions which salute mine Eys
A Gift from God I take:
The Earth, the Seas, the Light, the lofty Skies,
The Sun and Stars are mine; if these I prize.

A Stranger here,
Strange things doth meet, strange Glory see,
Strange Treasures lodg'd in this fair World appear,
Strange all and New to me:
But that they mine should be who Nothing was,
That Strangest is of all; yet brought to pass.

THOMAS TRAHERNE

There came to port last Sunday night
    The queerest little craft,
Without an inch of rigging on;

I looked and looked—and laughed!
It seemed so curious that she
        Should cross the Unknown water,
And moor herself within my room—
        My daughter! O my daughter!

GEORGE WASHINGTON CABLE

For So the Children Come

For so the children come
And so they have been coming.
Always in the same way they come
        born of the seed of man and woman.
No angels herald their beginnings.
No prophets predict their future courses.
No wisemen see a star to show where to find the babe
        that will save humankind.
Yet each night a child is born is a holy night,
Fathers and mothers—
        sitting beside their children's cribs
        feel glory in the sight of a new life beginning.
They ask, "Where and how will this new life end?
Or will it ever end?"

Each night a child is born is a holy night—
A time for singing,
A time for wondering,
A time for worshipping.

Sophia Lyon Fahs

On the Birth of a Child

Lo, to the battle-ground of Life,
    Child, you have come, like a conquering shout,
Out of a struggle—into strife;
    Out of a darkness—into doubt.

Girt with the fragile armor of youth,
    Child, you must ride into endless wars,
With the sword of protest, the buckler of truth,
    And a banner of love to sweep the stars.

About you the world's despair will surge;
    Into defeat you must plunge and grope.
Be to the faltering an urge;
    Be to the hopeless years a hope!

Be to the darkened world a flame;
    Be to its unconcern a blow—
For out of its pain and tumult you came,
    And into its tumult and pain you go.

LOUIS UNTERMEYER

Black Baby

The baby I hold in my arms is a black baby.
Today I set him in the sun and
Sunbeams danced on his head.

The baby I hold in my arms is a black baby.
I toil, and I cannot always cuddle him.
I place him on the ground at my feet.
He presses the warm earth with his hands,
He lifts the sand and laughs to see
It flow through his chubby fingers.
I watch to discern which are his hands,
Which is the sand. . . .

The baby I hold in my arms is a black baby.
Today the coal-man brought me coal.
Sixteen dollars a ton is the price I pay for coal.—

Costly fuel . . . though they say:
—If it is buried deep enough and lies hidden long enough
'Twill be no longer coal but diamonds. . . .
My black baby looks at me.
His eyes are like coals,
They shine like diamonds.

ANITA SCOTT COLEMAN

Spring

Sound the flute!
Now it's mute!
Birds delight,
Day and night,
Nightingale,
In the dale,
Lark in sky,—
Merrily,
Merrily, merrily to welcome in the year.

Little boy,
Full of joy;
Little girl,
Sweet and small;

Cock does crow,
So do you;
Merry voice,
Infant noise;
Merrily, merrily to welcome in the year.

Little lamb,
Here I am;
Come and lick
My white neck;
Let me pull
Your soft wool;
Let me kiss
Your soft face;
Merrily, merrily to welcome in the year.

WILLIAM BLAKE

Babyhood

What is the little one thinking about?
Very wonderful things, no doubt!
Unwritten history!
Unfathomed mystery!

Yet he laughs and cries, and eats and drinks,
And chuckles and crows, and nods and winks,
As if his head were as full of kinks
And curious riddles as any sphinx!

JOSIAH GILBERT HOLLAND

To Charlotte Pulteney

Timely blossom, Infant fair,
Fondling of a happy pair,
Every morn and every night
Their solicitous delight,
Sleeping, waking, still at ease,
Pleasing, without skill to please;
Little gossip, blithe and hale,
Tattling many a broken tale,
Singing many a tuneless song,
Lavish of a heedless tongue,
Simple maiden, void of art,
Babbling out the very heart,
Yet abandon'd to thy will,
Yet imagining no ill,
Yet too innocent to blush;
Like the linnet in the bush,
To the mother-linnet's note

Moduling her slender throat;
Chirping forth thy pretty joys;
Wanton in the change of toys,
Like the linnet green, in May,
Flitting to each bloomy spray;
Wearied then, and glad of rest,
Like the linnet in the nest:—
This thy present happy lot,
This, in time, will be forgot:
Other pleasures, other cares,
Ever-busy Time prepares;
And thou shalt in thy daughter see
This picture once resembl'd thee.

AMBROSE PHILIPS

To see helpless infancy stretching out her hands, and pouring out her cries in testimony of dependence, without any powers to alarm jealousy, or any guilt to alienate affection, must surely awaken tenderness in every human mind; and tenderness once excited will be hourly increased by the natural contagion of felicity, by the repercussion of communicated pleasure, by the consciousness of the dignity of benefaction.

SAMUEL JOHNSON

Étude Réaliste

A baby's feet, like sea-shells pink,
    Might tempt, should heaven see meet,
An angel's lips to kiss, we think,
    A baby's feet.

Like rose-hued sea-flowers toward the heat
    They stretch and spread and wink
Their ten soft buds that part and meet.

No flower-bells that expand and shrink
    Gleam half so heavenly sweet
As shine on life's untrodden brink
    A baby's feet.

A baby's hands, like rosebuds furled
    Whence yet no leaf expands,
Ope if you touch, though close upcurled,
    A baby's hands.

Then, fast as warriors grip their brands
    When battle's bolt is hurled,
They close, clenched hard like tightening bands.

No rosebuds yet by dawn impearled
    Match, even in loveliest lands,
The sweetest flowers in all the world—
    A baby's hands.

A baby's eyes, ere speech begin,
    Ere lips learn words or sighs,
Bless all things bright enough to win
    A baby's eyes.

Love, while the sweet thing laughs and lies,
    And sleep flows out and in,
Sees perfect in them Paradise.

Their glance might cast out pain and sin,
    Their speech make dumb the wise,
By mute glad godhead felt within
    A baby's eyes.

ALGERNON CHARLES SWINBURNE

Home and the Baby

Home was never home before,
  Till the baby came.
Love no golden jewels wore,
  Till the baby came.
There was joy, but now it seems
Dreams were not the rosy dreams,
Sunbeams not such golden beams—
  Till the baby came.

Home was never really gay,
  Till the baby came.
I'd forgotten how to play,
  Till the baby came.
Smiles were never half so bright,
Troubles never half so light,
Worry never took to flight,
  Till the baby came.

Home was never half so blest,
  Till the baby came.
Lacking something that was best,
  Till the baby came.

Kisses were not half so sweet,
Love not really so complete,
Joy had never found our street
Till the baby came.

EDGAR ALBERT GUEST

Standing by the crib of one's own baby, with that world-old pang of compassion and protectiveness toward this so little creature that has all its course to run, the heart flies back in yearning and gratitude to those who felt just so toward one's self. Then for the first time one understands the homely succession of sacrifices and pains by which life is transmitted and fostered down the stumbling generations of men.

CHRISTOPHER MORLEY

Find Out

Drool. Open your guppy mouth and stare. Eat the leaves on the palm tree. Chew on the corner of your book. Reach for forgotten toys under the chair and suck on them. Put everything into your mouth, even Daddy's wedding ring. Crinkle your baby brow and scowl at the funny-tasting cereal. Give your taste buds an adventure.

Find out what's savory, tangy, sweet, and sour.

Yank the CDs from the shelf. Kick your feet. Slap your bath water. Toss your blocks. Wriggle out of your pants. Shovel food into your ears, drop crumbs at your feet, and spill your juice. Tug my earring. Pull my hair. Pinch my nose. Grab my necklace and poke my teeth. Discover the wonders of your arms and fingers and legs and toes.

Find out what you can make them do.

Giggle at the wind-up toy. Rattle your jingle bells. Clang your music box. Gurgle and make bubbles. Jabber your baby-speak. Coo and squeal at will. Sing your songs.

Find out how to make important proclamations.

Gaze wide-eyed at the music makers. Stop hushed-still, and watch mommy's mouth as she sings. Teeter on your almost-balanced feet and try to catch sight of the barking dogs. Snap your head toward the music and listen. Squint at the sun. Sneeze. Watch the palm fronds dance. Hear the music; see the beauty.

Find out what fills you with joy.

Discover how your beautiful planet works, and learn what you can do in it now. Someday you'll be too grown-up to squish your food through your fingers, crawl under the dog, or utter nonsense syllables.

Find out, my baby grandson, my treasure, what I already know: the marvel that is you.

And when you're tired, little one, snuggle gently on the soft murmur of my heart. Rest your tiny cheek against my shoulder. Wrap your soft, baby arms around my neck so closely that your whisper-breath sings to me a lullaby. I'll rock you to sleep. Slumber softly and dream your baby dreams.

ELOISE VOLCKMANN SEARL

Sweet dreams, form a shade
O'er my lovely infant's head!
Sweet dreams of pleasant streams
By happy, silent, moony beams!

Sweet Sleep, with soft down
Weave thy brows an infant crown!
Sweet Sleep, angel mild,
Hover o'er my happy child!

Sweet smiles, in the night
Hover over my delight!
Sweet smiles, mother's smiles,
All the livelong night beguiles.

Sweet moans, dovelike sighs,
Chase not slumber from thy eyes!
Sweet moans, sweeter smiles,
All the dovelike moans beguiles.

Sleep, sleep, happy child!
All creation slept and smiled.
Sleep, sleep, happy sleep,
While o'er thee thy mother weep.

WILLIAM BLAKE

God bless little babies—with faces bright
Their tiny hands that wave and grasp the air
The random silk-like down they have for hair
Their eyes wide-wonder-lit at each new sight
And yes, their crying, even in the night:
Bless them because they are *both* joy and care
And for the thrilling heart-tugs that they share
Which makes us laugh or weep from pure delight.

ROSCOE TRUEBLOOD

You are my one, and I have not another;
Sleep soft, my darling, my trouble and treasure;
Sleep warm and soft in the arms of your mother,
Dreaming of pretty things, dreaming of pleasure.

CHRISTINA ROSSETTI

Where Shall the Baby's Dimple Be?

Over the cradle a mother hung,
Softly crooning a slumber song;
And these were the simple words she sung
All the evening long:

"Cheek or chin, or knuckle or knee,
Where shall the baby's dimple be?
Where shall the angel's finger rest
When he comes down to the baby's nest?
Where shall the angel's touch remain
When he awakens my babe again?"

Still as she bent and sang so low, a murmur into her music broke;
And she paused to hear, for she could but know the baby's angel spoke:

"Cheek or chin, or knuckle or knee,
Where shall the baby's dimple be?
Where shall my finger fall and rest
When I comes down to the baby's nest?
Where shall my fingers touch remain
When I awaken your babe again?"

Silent the mother sat, and dwelt, long in the sweet delay of choice;
And then by her baby's side she knelt, and sang with pleasant voice:

"Not on the limb, O angel dear!
For the charm with it's youth will disappear;
Not on the cheek shall the dimple be,
For the harboring smile will fade and flee;
But touch thou the chin with an impress deep,
And my baby the angel's seal shall keep."

JOSIAH GILBERT HOLLAND

Look! how he laughs and stretches out his arms,
And opens wide his blue eyes upon thine,
To hail his father; while his little form
Flutters as winged with joy. Talk not of pain!
The childless cherubs well might envy thee
The pleasures of a parent.

GEORGE GORDON LORD BYRON

Making the decision to have a child—it's momentous. It is to decide
forever to have your heart go walking outside your body.

ELIZABETH STONE

Roots and Wings

There are two lasting bequests we can give our children. One is roots. The other is wings.

HODDING CARTER, JR.

One of the most important things for our young people to learn is the difficult art of being at home in the world. Ahead of them lies the gigantic, but infinitely rewarding, task of learning to know and understand other peoples, and the equally difficult task of helping other peoples to know and understand them.

ELEANOR ROOSEVELT

Everything Possible

We have cleared off the table, the leftovers saved,
Washed the dishes and put them away
I have told you a story and tucked you in tight
At the end of your knockabout day
As the moon sets its sails to carry you to sleep
Over the midnight sea
I will sing you a song no one sang to me
May it keep you good company.

You can be anybody you want to be,
You can love whomever you will
You can travel any country where your heart leads
And know I will love you still
You can live by yourself, you can gather friends around,
You can choose one special one
And the only measure of your words and your deeds
Will be the love you leave behind when you're done.

There are girls who grow up strong and bold
There are boys quiet and kind
Some race on ahead, some follow behind
Some go in their own way and time
Some women love women, some men love men
Some raise children, some never do
You can dream all the day never reaching the end
Of everything possible for you.

Don't be rattled by names, by taunts, by games
But seek out spirits true
If you give your friends the best part of yourself
They will give the same back to you.

Fred Small

On Children

And a woman who held a babe against her bosom said,
"Speak to us of Children."

And he said:

Your children are not your children.

They are the sons and daughters of Life's
longing for itself.

They come through you but not from
you,

And though they are with you yet they
belong not to you.

You may give them your love but not
your thoughts,

For they have their own thoughts.

You may house their bodies but not
their souls,

For their souls dwell in the house of tomorrow,
which you cannot visit, not even in your dreams.

You may strive to be like them, but seek
not to make them like you.

For life goes not backward nor tarries
with yesterday.

You are the bows from which your children
as living arrows are sent forth.

The archer sees the mark upon the path
of the infinite, and He bends you with His
might that His arrows may go swift and far.

Let your bending in the archer's hand
be for gladness;

For even as He loves the arrow that flies,
so He loves also the bow that is stable.

KAHLIL GIBRAN

He that hath wife and children hath given hostages to fortune.

FRANCIS BACON

The Tao gives birth to all of creation.
The virtue of Tao in nature nurtures them,
and their family give them their form.
Their environment then shapes them into completion.
That is why every creature honors the Tao and its virtue.

No one tells them to honor the Tao and its virtue,
it happens all by itself.
So the Tao gives them birth,
and its virtue cultivates them,
cares for them,
nurtures them,
gives them a place of refuge and peace,
helps them to grow and shelters them.

It gives them life without wanting to possess them,
and cares for them expecting nothing in return.
It is their master, but it does not seek to dominate them.
This is called the dark and mysterious virtue.

LAO TZU

I love these little people; and it is not a slight thing when they, who are so fresh from God, love us.

CHARLES DICKENS

The Children's Hour

Between the dark and the daylight,
　　When the night is beginning to lower,
Comes a pause in the day's occupations,
　　That is known as the Children's Hour.

I hear in the chamber above me
　　The patter of little feet,
The sound of a door that is opened,
　　And voices soft and sweet.

From my study I see in the lamplight,
　　Descending the broad hall stair,
Grave Alice, and laughing Allegra,
　　And Edith with golden hair.

A whisper, and then a silence:
　　Yet I know by their merry eyes
They are plotting and planning together
　　To take me by surprise.

A sudden rush from the stairway,
    A sudden raid from the hall!
By three doors left unguarded
    They enter my castle wall!

They climb up into my turret
    O'er the arms and back of my chair;
If I try to escape, they surround me;
    They seem to be everywhere.

They almost devour me with kisses,
    Their arms about me entwine,
Till I think of the Bishop of Bingen
    In his Mouse-Tower on the Rhine!

Do you think, o blue-eyed banditti,
    Because you have scaled the wall,
Such an old mustache as I am
    Is not a match for you all!

I have you fast in my fortress,
    And will not let you depart,
But put you down into the dungeon
    In the round-tower of my heart.

And there will I keep you forever,
   Yes, forever and a day,
Till the walls shall crumble to ruin,
   And moulder in dust away!

HENRY WADSWORTH LONGFELLOW

He was almost three years old, and he was looking deep into a splendid red peony. He was greatly alive to himself (though he had not yet learned to think of himself as Francis) and the peony, in its fashion, was also greatly alive to itself, and the two looked at each other from their very different egotisms with solemn self-confidence.

The little boy nodded at the peony and the peony seemed to nod back. The little boy was neat, clean, and pretty. The peony was unchaste, disheveled as peonies must be, and at the height of its beauty. It was a significant moment, for it was Francis's first conscious encounter with beauty—beauty that was to be the delight, the torment, and the bitterness of his life—but except for Francis himself, and perhaps the peony, nobody knew of it, or would have heeded if they had known. Every hour is filled with such moments, big with significance for someone.

ROBERTSON DAVIES

won't you celebrate with me

won't you celebrate with me
what i have shaped into
a kind of life? i had no model.
born in babylon
both nonwhite and woman
what did i see to be except myself?
i made it up
here on this bridge between
starshine and clay,
my one hand; come celebrate
with me that everyday
something has tried to kill me
and has failed.

LUCILLE CLIFTON

Declaration of the Rights of the Child

All children have the right to what follows, no matter what their race, colour sex, language, religion, political or other opinion, or where they were born or who they were born to.

You have the special right to grow up and to develop physically and spiritually in a healthy and normal way, free and with dignity.

67

You have a right to a name and to be a member of a country.

You have a right to special care and protection and to good food, housing and medical services.

You have the right to special care if handicapped in any way.

You have the right to love and understanding, preferably from parents and family, but from the government where these cannot help.

You have the right to go to school for free, to play, and to have an equal chance to develop yourself and to learn to be responsible and useful. Your parents have special responsibilities for your education and guidance.

You have the right always to be among the first to get help.

You have the right to be protected against cruel acts or exploitation, e.g., you shall not be obliged to do work which hinders your development both physically and mentally. You should not work before a minimum age and never when that would hinder your health, and your moral and physical development.

You should be taught peace, understanding, tolerance, and friendship among all people.

ADAPTED FROM UNITED NATIONS

On Hearing of the Sadness of the Slave-Children
from the Fear of Being Sold

When children play the livelong day,
Like birds and butterflies;
As free and gay, sport time away,
And know not car or sights
Then all the air seems fresh and fair
Around us and above.
Life's flowers are there; and everywhere
Is innocence and love.
When children play with fear all day,
A blight must be at hand.
Then joy decays, and birds of prey
Are hovering o'er the land.
When young hearts weep as they go to sleep,
Then all the world is sad.
The flesh must creep, and woes are deep,
When children are not glad.

ELIZA CABOT FOLLEN

Save the children
Tortured by hunger and thirst
Ravaged by preventable disease
victimized by violence, savaged by the brutalities of war.
Save the children.

Protect the children
Stunted by suffering
deprived of beauty, joy, laughter
denied freedom, justice and peace
Thwarted by limitation due to race, religion,
age, sex, class, or caste.
Protect the children.

Care for the children
Nurtured by love, upheld by guidance
uplifted by understanding
Care for the children.
Enriched by a safe and healthy environment
empowered by education, challenged by opportunity, and
    strengthened by the fullness of rights

Care for the children.
Enhanced by taking their place in a global family
and enriched by differences
Care for the children.

Children are life and miracle, beauty, and mystery
fulfillment and promise.
Save the children.
Protect the children.
Care for the children.
May it be so.

ADAPTED FROM WORLD RELIGIOUS LEADERS

May we never rest until every child of earth in every generation
is free from all prisons of the mind
and of the body
and of the spirit,
until the earth and the hills and the seas shall dance
and the universe itself resound with the joyful cry:
"Behold! I am!"

JOHN CUMMINS

Can a father see his child
Weep, nor be with sorrow filled?

Can a mother sit and hear
An infant groan, an infant fear?

No, no! never can it be!
Never, never can it be!

WILLIAM BLAKE

The joys of parents are secret; and so are their griefs and fears.

FRANCIS BACON

It is a wise father that knows his own child.

WILLIAM SHAKESPEARE

Columbus Cheney

This weeping willow!
Why do you not plant a few
For the millions of children not yet born,
As well as for us?
Are they not non-existent, or cells asleep
Without mind?

Or do they come to earth, their birth
Rupturing the memory of previous being?
Answer! The field of unexplored intuition is yours.
But in any case why not plant willows for them,
As well as for us?

EDGAR LEE MASTERS

Grandparents have a special responsibility in the nurturing of children. You taught your own daughters and sons what it means to be a parent, your grandchildren will probably turn to you when they are not quite pleased with how their parents are doing their job. Such is traditionally the way of grandchildren and grandparents, and all in all, it is a good and happy way.

As you love your grandchildren, remember also your love for your own child and for your child's partner. Respect them for the choices they have made, support them in their work as parents, assist them so far as you are able, and above all trust them to do well the work that you have done in your own time. At the same time, rejoice in the special, sacred relationship that exists in love between grandparent and grandchild.

LINDSAY BATES

Throughout their lives, your task for these children is to be their comforters and adult friends, advisors, and "parents in reserve"— grownups who can be trusted to help them through the rough times that are an inevitable part of growing up.

We ask you to help teach these children, through your example and your words, to know that this world is their home, that it is holy, that their lives are each a special gift to themselves and to all who love them. It is your particular task to help them learn that the power of love and creation that guides the universe is stronger than all hatred and sorrow. Teach them to know the sanctity of life, the holiness of integrity, the virtue of charity, and the challenge of faith. At the same time, offer to their parents that same support and love, assisting them in their most difficult, most joyful work.

LINDSAY BATES

Ask any parent and they will tell you that life changes with the birth of a child. The life that was—is no longer. One life ends and a new one begins, one that centers on the well-being of a vulnerable and dependent child. Even parents who have furnished a nursery with all the necessary equipment—a crib, warm blankets, colorful and cuddly toys, diapers, and a soft, safe environment for a child to explore— can find themselves unprepared for the larger realities of parenting.

Children are demanding. Their needs can sometimes seem unending. While the relationship between parent and child may be based on mutual affection, it is neither equal nor reciprocal. Children are dependent on parents for their very survival. They are vulnerable in a way parents are not. The job of parents is to meet the needs of their children; it is not the job of children to meet the needs of their parents.

That's not to say that raising children doesn't meet some deep needs. For example, the satisfaction that comes from the dedication required to raise children into caring adults, or the joy that comes from their laughter, or the feel of their tiny arms offering an affectionate hug. These are the tender joys that come with having children present in our lives, the unexpected gifts they bring to us.

Children are precious gifts, but there is no doubt that they come with a burden of responsibility. They cannot care for themselves, so we must care for them, and we must do so in a way that empowers them to eventually take responsibility for their own lives.

When we behold a child, we behold the future. How that future is shaped depends on the lives we create for our children now.

DIANE DOWGIERT

All of the central opportunities of a classic spiritual life are available in the walk with children, if we can open our eyes to see them. We are called to hold love at the center of what we do. We are called to study and practice patience, forgiveness, crime and punishment, power, suffering, grace, creation, and relinquishment. How could this not be a spiritual path? It's there for us very clearly when our children are babies and young children, but it doesn't seem to disappear even when they're in their fifties. Our influence decreases or even vanishes, but our urgent concern for our children never leaves us, and the role of mother or father stays with us until the day we die. I have also long realized that aunts and uncles and friends of the family play parenting roles often and well. The spiritual path with children is available to all of us, whether or not we give birth, as long as we choose to be a committed figure in a child's life.

KATHLEEN MCTIGUE

I was playing Legos with a four-year-old a few years ago. He was building a plane, and he wanted me to make one too. After a while I asked him what the flat yellow Legos that were protruding far from the front of the plane were for. "Oh, those are the beds so the pilot can nap." Right. The four year old mind at work. Not something I would have thought of—giving the pilot a place to sleep and putting those quarters *outside* the plane itself. I sat there a bit incredulous. When I was his age I loved to build flying machines out of Legos too. And they were filled with flights of fancy like his plane was—I seem to recall one of my special planes having a swimming pool. Not too practical. This memory relieved me: Yes! At one time I too had a creative, outside-the-box mind like his. And I was a little sad too: It seems the grown up me has way too many rules getting in the way. Growing up killed off some of my creativity.

JENNIFER O'QUILL

We don't hear stories about saints and sages walking the path to their enlightenment hauling bags of diapers and stacks of diaper wipes, mini-packs of tissues, liquid Tylenol, and teething rings. It's hard to imagine them engaging in soul-deepening religious thought or dialogue while they wipe a runny nose or clean up after SpaghettiOs. And a parent is more likely to be found poring time and again over the words of *The Runaway Bunny* or *Goodnight Moon* than over the classic sacred texts.

The real journey with children is motivated not by our spiritual hungers but by our offsprings' more prosaic appetites. Although children's lovely, spontaneous ways may re-awaken us to the world, being a parent often doesn't look anything like traveling a spiritual path. Parents have little opportunity for regular prayer or meditation, Sabbath reflection, study, or journal-writing. Instead, such practices may be reduced and disrupted almost to the vanishing point. The real journey for parents leads right through the life we are living— through the chaos, the interruptions, and the exhaustion.

This ordinary, unsung path requires tremendous openness to the unanticipated. It meanders around a thousand turns that feel like detours or dead ends. It requires faith that the spirit does not grow in a straight line; nor does it require traditional forms and practices, as helpful as these can be. Real spiritual growth depends on our willingness to be transformed. And very little transforms us as thoroughly as sharing our lives with children.

KATHLEEN MCTIGUE

May we be grateful for the gift of children in our lives.

Though we cannot save them from trials or sorrow,
we can show how much we love them.

Though we cannot make them into people of our choosing,
we can be generous with positive recognition
and celebrate their triumphs and support what is unique and special.

As they learn from their time with us, so shall we learn from them
as we anticipate the day when they shall stand with us,
challenging us and offering us a new companionship.

CHERYL JACK

I want our children to develop what I call critical inquiry,
    the capacity to think critically
    and inquire out of a sense of genuine interest.
I want our children to learn of the inspiring heritage we have.
I want our children to know there is indeed hope in the world,
    that there are morals,
    that there is such a thing as right and wrong,
    and that there are differing degrees of rightness and wrongdoing.
I want our children to become human beings
    of compassion, achievement, integrity, and discipline.
I want our children to learn how to make good decisions,
    drawing on the authority of personal experience,
    the authority of reason,
    and the authority of tradition.
I want our children to know where we human beings have failed
    and to have the hope that we can move forward.
I want our children to learn they are the authors of their lives,
    that they are free to explore the wide wonders of the world,
    free to compose their lives as the seed within them dictates.
I want to dare our children to be creative
    rather than passively accept the world
    "just the way things are."
I want our children to discern what is truly important to them.
Finally, I want to spark our children's imaginations,

so they may dream and envision a world
that is better than the one we've got
so they can bring it into being.
I want all of these because I believe that in each child and adult
there lies dormant life's longing for itself.

ALAN TAYLOR

When my children go to bed I meet them in their bedroom and communicate two things to them—one using American Sign Language and one in spoken English.

I would like to think that hearing me repeat this simple message every night before falling asleep will help them to develop a healthy spiritual perspective. I know that it has helped me enormously in my spiritual development. It helps remind me of what I believe and reestablishes a connection with my children every night, no matter what has happened during the day. And it helps prepare me, as well as my children, for the "little death" of sleep.

After tucking them in, I sign, You, my daughters. You, big sister and little sister. You. Beautiful, strong, and brave. I love you. Play finished. Time to sleep now. Good night. You, good girls.

And then I say out loud:

You are very welcome here on this planet and in this family. You are healthy and strong. You are strong and brave. I am very glad you

decided to be born and to be my daughters, so I can be your daddy.
You have some important things to learn in this life, and it is your
job to learn them. You have some important things to do in this life,
and it is your job to figure out what they are so you can do them.
You are also here to have fun and to learn how to love. I love you
and I am proud of you.

GREGORY L. NOONEY

Position available: parent. Qualifications: none. Position is open to
anybody regardless of age, experience, intention, motivation, willingness, preparation, or desire. The job will consist of making one or
more children the center of your life for the remainder of your life.
You will be expected to provide financial support, housing, clothing,
sustenance, education, moral values, entertainment, limits, ideas, and
boundless love. You will encourage your children to learn to walk, so
that they can walk, then run, and then drive away. You will teach
them to talk so that, very soon, they can tell you "No!" in a thousand
different ways. In spite of the fact that you have agreed to take them
into the very core of your heart and mind, the main expectation of
this position is that you let them go—sometimes gradually, sometimes
abruptly. Pay: Ha, ha. Benefits: Smiles, hugs, tears, gratitude, the
opportunity to know fully and unabashedly what you did to your
own parents, the opportunity to do things differently from your own

parents, the opportunity to make the same mistakes your own parents made—and other, bigger and better mistakes, the profoundly moving experience of seeing your child smile, laugh, cry, fail, succeed, grow, change, surprise you, aggravate you, love you, and leave you.

ROBERTA FINKELSTEIN

In my dealing with my child, my Latin and Greek, my accomplishments and my money stead me nothing, but as much soul as I have avails.

RALPH WALDO EMERSON

Honi ha-Ma'aggel once saw on his travels an old man planting a carob tree. He asked him when he thought the tree would bear fruit. "After seventy years," was the reply.

"Dost thou expect to live seventy years and eat the fruit of thy labor?"

"I did not find the world desolate when I entered it," said the old man, "and as my fathers planted for me before I was born, so do I plant for those who will come after me."

TALMUD

Giving birth and nourishing,
making without possessing,
expecting nothing in return.
To grow, yet not to control:
This is the mysterious virtue.

LAO TZU

What Rules the World

Blessings on the hand of women!
Angels guard its strength and grace,
In the palace, cottage, hovel,
Oh, no matter where the place;
Would that never storms assailed it,
Rainbows ever gently curled;
For the hand that rocks the cradle
Is the hand that rules the world.

Infancy's the tender fountain,
Power may with beauty flow,
Mother's first to guide the streamlets,
From them souls unresting grow-
Grow on for the good or evil,

Sunshine streamed or evil hurled;
For the hand that rocks the cradle
Is the hand that rules the world.

Woman, how divine your mission
Here upon our natal sod!
Keep, oh, keep the young heart open
Always to the breath of God!
All true trophies of the ages
Are from mother-love impearled;
For the hand that rocks the cradle
Is the hand that rules the world.

Blessings on the hand of women!
Fathers, sons, and daughters cry,
And the sacred song is mingled
With the worship in the sky—
Mingles where no tempest darkens,
Rainbows evermore are hurled;
For the hand that rocks the cradle
Is the hand that rules the world.

WILLIAM ROSS WALLACE

What we owe you, our children, is our best effort to be a person worth emulating and to send through our lives a message to the future we hope you will feel is worth transmitting to your children and grandchildren. I hope I can grow big enough one day to feel I have done that.

MARIAN WRIGHT EDELMAN

Children are a treasure, the wealth of any country. They are the future leaders of society and the entire nation. But in order to play that role they must be given support. They must be given education. Their health must be looked after. And, above all, they must be given love.

NELSON MANDELA

Parenting is a ministry of love—an expression of unconditional love for your children and trust in the universal presence of love as a guiding force in the world. From the power of love, parents gain the strength and courage to make decisions (popular and unpopular, easy and heartbreakingly hard) day in and day out, without ever knowing if they are right or wrong, or what the future consequence might be.

BETSY HILL WILLIAMS

Of course, parents, first and foremost, are responsible for their children. But we are all responsible for ensuring that children are raised in a nation that doesn't just talk about family values, but acts in ways that values families. Just think . . . we are all part of one family, the American family, and each one of us has value. Each child who comes into this world should feel special—every boy and every girl.

HILLARY CLINTON

If children grow up with the consciousness that their community consists of just Mama and Papa, and then they have to deal with a problem that they alone cannot solve, they will have no-one outside the family to whom they can turn. The parents and only the parents are responsible for what the child makes of itself, and that is too much to ask from two people. Often it is in fact only one parent who has to do it all.

If children are given a wider concept of community, they will not have to be at the mercy of just one person. The child can then seek out another, to whom he wants to turn, and if this person doesn't help him then he can go to the next. Since we are all only people, we all have our limits as to what we can do and what we are able to give. To raise children we are always dependent upon the support of others.

As we say in our village, "It needs a whole village to raise a child."
And it is just as true to say that it needs a whole village to look after
the emotional health of the parents.

The Child

See yon blithe child that dances in our sight!
Can gloomy shadows fall from one so bright?
    Fond mother, whence these fears?
While buoyantly he rushes o'er the lawn,
Dream not of clouds to stain his manhood's dawn,
    Nor dim that sight with tears.

No cloud he spies in brightly glowing hours,
But feels as if the newly vested bowers
    For him could never fade:
Too well we know that vernal pleasures fleet,
But having him, so gladsome, fair, and sweet,
    Our loss is overpaid.

Amid the balmiest flowers that earth can give
Some bitter drops distil, and all that live
    A mingled portion share;

87

But, while he learns these truths which we lament,
Such fortitude as ours will sure be sent,
    Such solace to his care.

SARA COLERIDGE

You are aware that it is the beginning of any undertaking which is
the most important part—especially for anything young and tender?
That is the time when each individual thing can be most easily
moulded, and receive whatever mark you want to impress upon it
. . . . Shall we be perfectly content, then, to let our children listen to
any old stories, made up by any old storytellers? Shall we let them
open their minds to beliefs which are the opposite, for the most part,
of those we think they should hold when they grow up?

PLATO

Here is a thing my heart wishes the world had more of:
I heard it in the air of one night when I listened
To a mother singing softly to a child restless and angry in the darkness.

CARL SANDBURG

In the old tales, the birth of a special child occasioned the arrival of supernatural beings (fairy godmothers, guardian spirits) bearing magical gifts. The gifts that we flesh and blood parents have to offer our children are no less magical. They will be needed, not because our children ride off on mythical quests, but—more important—because we want them to grow to be whole and loving people in a real world. In so doing, we know that a child will "climb to the highest heavens," and test not only "the furthest limits of the sea," but the limits of life itself.

ANONYMOUS

But a child who has been treated with real respect, who has a feeling that his elders expect certain standards even from a young member of the family, will behave with astonishing maturity. A child who feels the basic acceptance that goes with respect, and knows he is trusted because he is accepted, will achieve remarkable ability in acquiring self-control and consideration for others.

ELEANOR ROOSEVELT

In a house which becomes a home, one hands down and another takes up the heritage of mind and heart, laughter and tears, musings and deeds.

Love, like a carefully loaded ship, crosses the gulf between the generations.

Let us bring up our children. It is not the place of some official to hand to them their heritage.

If others impart to our children our knowledge and ideals, they will lose all of us that is wordless and full of wonder.

Let us build memories in our children, lest they drag out joyless lives, lest they allow treasures to be lost because they have not been given the keys.

We live, not by things, but by the meanings of things. It is needful to transmit the passwords from generation to generation.

ANTOINE DE SAINT-ÉXUPÉRY

Think about times you've experienced the passing of love and values from generation to generation or from one person to another—not just at ritual times but at any time. There's usually nothing fancy or extraordinary about it. We do it in all kinds of different ways at different times. Often we don't even know we are doing it. We are like honeybees transporting pollen from flower to flower.

I remember my grandmother making tapioca just the way I liked it, and then letting me mix in Welch's grape jelly. If you think tapioca pudding looks a little strange, think of purple tapioca pudding. But I loved it, and her willingness to please her grandchild in this harmless way was one way of passing love from generation to generation.

I remember learning that my grandfather was always a little early to appointments. And as I've thought about that in the years since it seems to me like a way that he honored the person he'd agreed to meet at a particular time. Another password from generation to generation.

And I could make a long list of what I've learned from and absorbed from my father and my mother through their examples and their consistent acts of kindness and responsibility and love.

And then there are the mentors and teachers in my life, another long list.

And it's not that any of these people were or are perfect, but they each shared their love and taught their values.

Even people I've barely known have had their effect on my life. My grandfather died when I was about nine or ten years old, and I remember standing outside the church after the service in my little checked jacket and tie. A man I didn't even know came up to me and offered a word of sympathy. At the time it felt awkward to me. But I've remembered, haven't I?

KEN READ-BROWN

I think it is essential that you should teach your child that he has an intellectual and a spiritual obligation to decide for himself what he thinks and not to allow himself to accept what comes from others without putting it through his own reasoning process.

ELEANOR ROOSEVELT

Among the most accomplished and fabled tribes of Africa, no tribe was considered to have warriors more fearsome or more intelligent than the mighty Masai. It is perhaps surprising then to learn the traditional greeting that passed between Masai warriors. "Kasserian ingera?" one would always say to another. It means, "How are the children?" It is still the traditional greeting among the Masai, acknowledging the high value that the Masai always place on their children's well-being. Even warriors with no children of their own would always give the traditional answer, "All the children are well," meaning that peace and safety prevail, that the priorities of protecting the young, the powerless, are in place; that Masai society has not forgotten its reason for being, its proper functions and responsibilities. "All the children are well" means that life is good. It means that the daily struggles of existence do not preclude proper caring for their young. I wonder how it might affect our own cultures if we took to greeting each other with this daily question: "And how are the children?" I wonder, if we heard that question and passed it along to each other a dozen times a day, whether it would begin to make a difference in how children are thought of and cared for in our own country. I wonder if every adult among us, parent and non-parent alike, would feel an equal responsibility for the daily care and protection of all the children in our community, in our town, in our state, in our country. I wonder if we could truly say without any hesitation, "The children are well. Yes, all the children are well."

PATRICIA HOERTDOERFER

There can be no more important calling than raising healthy and hopeful children and grandchildren—quite a challenge in these times. First, we must heal ourselves and make our lives upright. Then we must give our progeny all the love, patience, stability, and effort we can summon from within ourselves. Here is to healing and new hope for our lives and for all those whom we touch.

CAROLYN S. OWEN-TOWLE

There is a wonderful word, why?, that children use. All children. When they stop using it, the reason, too often, is that no one bothered to answer them, no one tried to keep alive one of the most important attributes a person can have: interest in the world around him. No one fostered and cultivated the child's innate sense of the adventure of life. One of the things I believe most intensely is that every child's *why* should be answered with care—and with respect.

ELEANOR ROOSEVELT

Do you remember yourself as child? When you were an infant, the one who held and fed you was your whole world, your God, with all power and all knowledge. If you had been totally deprived of that kind of nurture, you would have failed to thrive. Your curiosity about the world led you to examine specks of dust in sunlight or crumbs on the floor, your toes, and everything within reach. As you grew, you learned most naturally through spontaneous play. Maybe you sang or danced, as children often do, unembarrassed by your audience. Maybe you explored the world of nature by playing in the rain or snow or bringing home a wounded animal. Maybe you acted out adult life with friends or with dolls and stuffed animals. These early experiences of self-expression and exploration of the real world formed the basis of your understanding about God, the universe, and everything.

KATHLEEN ELLIS

The Great End in Religious Instruction

The great end in religious instruction is not to stamp our minds upon the young, but to stir up their own;

Not to make them see with our eyes, but to look inquiringly and steadily with their own;

Not to give them a definite amount of knowledge, but to inspire a fervent love of truth;

Not to form an outward regularity, but to touch inward springs;

Not to bind them by ineradicable prejudices to our particular sect or peculiar notions, but to prepare them for impartial, conscientious judging of whatever subjects may be offered to their decision;

Not to burden the memory, but to quicken and strengthen the power of thought;

Not to impose religion upon them in the form of arbitrary rules, but to awaken the conscience, the moral discernment.

In a word, the great end in religious instruction is to awaken the soul, to excite and cherish spiritual life.

WILLIAM ELLERY CHANNING

Some beliefs are like walled gardens. They encourage exclusiveness, and the feeling of being especially privileged.

Other beliefs are expansive and lead the way into wider and deeper sympathies.

Some beliefs are like shadows, clouding children's days with fears of unknown calamities.

Other beliefs are like sunshine, blessing children with the warmth of happiness. . . .

Some beliefs are like binders, shutting off the power to choose one's own direction.

Other beliefs are like gateways opening wide vistas for exploration.

Some beliefs weaken a person's selfhood. They blight the growth of resourcefulness.

Other beliefs nurture self-confidence and enrich the feeling of personal worth.

Some beliefs are rigid, like the body of death, impotent in a changing world.

Other beliefs are pliable, like the young sapling, ever growing with the upward thrust of life.

SOPHIA LYON FAHS

Whether we wish it so or not, our children are religious, spiritual beings. From within their own magical selves they know feelings, intuitions, and impulses. From the people, stories, songs, and media of their environs they hear religious words and messages and see religious symbols and images. From the experiences of their daily living they encounter religious events. They see dry sticks sprout pulsing green leaves. They see the deer killed on the highway. They watch their teacher's tummy grow round with new life, and bid farewell to their uncle dying of AIDS. From the demands of their living and growing in the world they face situations that require from them a religious decision, response, or interpretation. We cannot choose whether they will be religious, but we can choose how and to what extent we will support, guide, and celebrate this dimension of their nature.

JEANNE HARRISON NIEUWEJAAR

Standing in the Dark

Remember, Father, when I was a very little girl
and afraid of the dark,
not because of bears and crocodiles
but because the sky was so wide,
and I called you from the living room,
golden with lamps and voices,
to save me from the hovering questions
that circled the ceiling above my bed:

> But how can the sky go on forever?
> And how many stars are there?
> And if the sky's shaped like a doughnut,
> who's holding the doughnut?
> And if we go to heaven when we die,
> how long will we live up there?
> And what does forever mean?

And you, after a long silence,
> stroking my hair: I don't know.
> None of us knows.
But your voice softened the dark
and I never knew when you left the room.

PAT KING

98

People were bringing little children to him in order that he might touch them; and the disciples spoke sternly to them. But when Jesus saw this, he was indignant and said to them, "Let the little children come to me; do not stop them; for it is to such as these that the kingdom of God belongs. Truly I tell you, whoever does not receive the kingdom of God as a little child will never enter it." And he took them up in his arms, laid his hands on them, and blessed them.

MARK 10:13–16

Blessed indeed is the man who hears many gentle voices call him father!

LYDIA MARIA CHILD

Of a Foolish Father

And there was a certain man that had a son whom he greatly loved. And he thought within himself saying, None is wise enough to instruct my son in the mysteries of the eternal: neither priest nor Levite shall tell him what is good and what is evil, lest his mind be corrupted with error. And he saith, This shall he do: he shall wait until he is a man, then he shall know of himself what to believe.

But it was not as the father thought. For the son did grow and was strong. Keepeth he his eyes open for seeing, and his ears for hearing. And his teachers were neither priests nor Levites. Neither did he come to the Temple for instruction. But his teachers were them that speaketh into the air, and them that were seen in the pictures of Babylon, and messengers in bright colors that were brought into the household on the morning of the Sabbath day.

And when the father was old he understood that the mind of his son had not been as an empty vessel that waiteth for a day to be filled, but that it was like unto a parched field that drinketh of that which falleth upon it.

CLINTON LEE SCOTT

I sincerely believe that for the child, and for the parent seeking to guide him, it is not half so important to *know* as to *feel*. If facts are the seeds that later produce knowledge and wisdom, then the emotions and the impressions of the senses are the fertile soil in which the seeds must grow. The years of early childhood are the time to prepare the soil.

RACHEL CARSON

What we remember from childhood we remember forever—permanent ghosts, stamped, imprinted, eternally seen.

CYNTHIA OZICK

All You of the Heavens

Sun, Moon, Stars, all you that move in the heavens, hear us!
Into your midst has come a new life.
Make his path smooth, that he may reach the brow of the first hill!

Winds, Clouds, Rain, Mist, all you that move in the air, hear us!
Into your midst has come a new life.
Make her path smooth, that she may reach the brow of the
    second hill!

Hills, Valleys, Rivers, Lakes, Trees, Grasses, all you of the earth,
    hear us!
Into your midst has come a new life.
Make his path smooth, that he may reach the brow of the third hill!

Birds, great and small, that fly in the air,
Animals, great and small, that dwell in the forest,
Insects that creep among the grasses and burrow in the ground,
    hear us!
Into your midst has come a new life.
Make her path smooth, that she may reach the brow of the fourth
    hill!

All you of the heavens, all you of the air, all you of the earth, hear us!
Into your midst has come a new life.
Make his path smooth, then shall he travel beyond the four hills!

OMAHA PRAYER

We ask ourselves, Who am I to be brilliant, gorgeous, talented, fabulous? Actually, who are you *not* to be? You are a child of God. . . . We are all meant to shine, as children do. We were born to make manifest the glory of God that is within us.

MARIANNE WILLIAMSON

When a child walks down the road, a company of angels goes before him proclaiming, "Make way for the image of the Holy One."

HASIDIC PROVERB

And Nature, the old nurse, took
    The child upon her knee,
Saying: "Here is a story-book
    Thy Father has written for thee."

"Come, wander with me," she said,
    "Into regions yet untrod;
And read what is still unread
    In the manuscripts of God."

HENRY WADSWORTH LONGFELLOW

The Divine Lullaby

    I hear Thy voice, dear Lord,
I hear it by the stormy sea,
    When winter nights are black and wild,
And when, affright, I call to Thee;
It calms my fears and whispers me,
    "Sleep well, my child."

    I hear Thy voice, dear Lord,
In singing winds, in falling snow,
    The curfew chimes, the midnight bell.

"Sleep well, my child," it murmurs low;
"The guardian angels come and go—
    O child, sleep well!"

    I hear Thy voice, dear Lord,
Aye, though the singing winds be stilled,
    Though hushed the tumult of the deep,
My fainting heart with anguish chilled
By Thy assuring tone is thrilled—
    "Fear not, and sleep!"

    Speak on—speak on, dear Lord!
And when the last dread night is near,
    With doubts and fears and terrors wild,
Oh, let my soul expiring hear
Only these words of heavenly cheer,
    "Sleep well, my child!"

EUGENE FIELD

To give someone a blessing is the most significant affirmation we can offer. It is more than a word of praise or appreciation; it is more than pointing out someone's talents or good deeds; it is more than putting someone in the light. To give a blessing is to affirm, to say "yes" to a person's Belovedness. And more than that: to give a blessing creates the reality of which it speaks. . . . A blessing goes beyond the distinction between admiration or condemnation, between virtues or vices, between good deeds or evil deeds. A blessing touches the original goodness of the other and calls for his or her Belovedness.

HENRI NOUWEN

I want to give you something to help express my deepest wish for you
—and to help you remember this moment.

I give you the gift of sugar,
representing life's sweetness.
I wish that for you in abundance.

I give you the gift of rice.
May your life bring forth many fruits
from even the smallest of seeds.

I give you a silver coin,
that in your life you may have all that you need
and even more to share.

I also give you the gift of white cotton,
    that you may live to become white-haired and wise.

Accept these gifts in the spirit of hope,
    that love may be transmitted across the generations.

ANTHONY DAVID

All things of tenderness and grace, bless our minds and lift us up
    forever.
All works of strength, bless our minds and lift us up forever.
All memories of love, bless our minds and lift us up forever.
Beautiful is the sight of many children at play:
Beautiful is the croon of mothers and fathers over a babe;
Beautiful are the feet and hands of the newborn.
All things of tenderness and grace, all works of strength, and
    memories of love,
    bless our minds and lift them up forever.

ELIZABETH M. STRONG

Choose Peace

You are my hope; our hope.

You are starting out fresh.
You have a chance to do it right.
    To listen to the voices.
    To accept the gifts.
    To love despite wrongs.
    You and your friends.

Although, like us, you will make mistakes, you can do better than we
    have.
    Choose peace.
    Choose justice.
    Choose compassion.
    Choose beauty.
    Choose love.

Our hopes and our dreams rest in you.
They are our gift.
Use them well.

PHYLLIS L. HUBBELL

Let us receive into our hearts all children.

Let us remember the children we once were and who still live within us. Let us love them now, in this quiet moment.

Let us remember the children of our own families and the children of our friends. Let us love them now, in the quiet of this moment.

Let us remember the children who are homeless,
    children who are separated from their families,
    children who are hungry or in pain,
    children whose lives are threatened
    by drugs, crime, and lack of health care.

Let us love them now, in the quiet of this moment.

Let us remember all children and commit ourselves to their growth and safety, their health and education, their uniqueness and their unfolding beauty. Let us love them now, in the quiet of this moment and forever more. Amen.

CONNIE STERNBERG

Watch over thy child, O Lord, as his days increase; bless and guide him wherever he may be, keeping him unspotted from the world. Strengthen him when he stands; comfort him when discouraged or sorrowful; raise him up if he fall; and in his heart may thy peace which passeth understanding abide all the days of his life; through Jesus Christ our Lord. Amen.

BOOK OF COMMON PRAYER

Merciful God,

    I thank thee for having with tender care protected this child in the mother's womb, and preserved it, in its helpless and defenceless condition, from all manner of danger and disease. I thank thee that, in darkness and in solitude, thou didst shape its limbs with artistic symmetry and beauty, and having furnished it with all necessary appliances, thou hast in the fullness of time brought it into the world, to do thy work and serve thy people. And as I thankfully bow before thee for this thy gift, which is unto me a fresh token of thy love, a treasure and a joy, grant that I may fully realise my responsibility and discharge my stewardship with fidelity. Conscious of my weakness and imperfections, I cast myself under thy guidance and most humbly do I beseech thee to give me faith, strength, and true paternal love, that I may, as thy devoted servant, keep this infant under thy guardianship and care, and rear it for thy service. Bless this child and be unto it Father, Mother and Friend, that it may ever repose on thy tender lap far from all evil. God of this house, make the newborn child a real joy in all things unto its parents and a blessing to the whole family. For all thy mercies, good God, we ascribe unto the glory everlasting.

KESHUB CHANDRA SEN

Sleep my child and peace attend thee,
All through the night
Guardian angels God will send thee,
All through the night
Soft the drowsy hours are creeping,
Hill and dale in slumber sleeping
I my loving vigil keeping,
All through the night.
Angels watching ever round thee,
All through the night.

HAROLD BOULTON

Spirit of life, watch my child when I cannot. Encircle her with love, protect her from a world which has become cynical. Knowing that I cannot stop time, not even for a moment, and freeze the picture of her from my window, let me hold her gently in my memory. Let all those children she once was remain joyful spirits enriching my reminiscences. Spirit of life, watch all our children. Keep them safe as they adventure toward adulthood, and let them turn and wave to us as they step out of our care and into the world of their making.

ELIZABETH TARBOX

Does it sound simple that children are born with potential and we just need the right conditions for the seed to grow? I don't mean to pretend that it is easy. We should dedicate ourselves to the greatest values expressed by human beings, but we need to acknowledge that it is not an easy task to put these values in place when we are bringing up children. We must continually revisit our values, restate and absorb them, make fresh starts, and find ways to strengthen ourselves in the face of difficulties. A belief in a Loving Spirit, the supporting ground of Being, which many call God, can be a great help. At the same time I acknowledge that there are people who are uncertain about such a belief in God, people who nonetheless put their faith in the values of love and kindness and nurture Beauty in our world. I can comfortably use the word *God*, but I know that this is not the same for everyone.

JUNE PETTITT

God make my life a little light,
Within the world to glow;
A tiny flame that burneth bright
Wherever I may go.

God make my life a little flower,
That giveth joy to all,
Content to bloom in native bower,
Although its place be small.

God make my life a little song,
That comforteth the sad,
That helpeth others to be strong,
And makes the singer glad.

God make my life a little staff,
Whereupon the weak may rest,
That so what health and strength I have,
May serve my neighbors best.

MATILDA B. B. EDWARDS

Our songs sing back to us something of our essence, something of
our truth, something of our uniqueness. When our songs are sung

back to us, it is not about approval, but about recognizing our being and our belonging in the human family.

It is good to know our songs by heart for those lonely times when the world is not singing them back to us. That's usually a good time to start humming to yourself that song that is most your own.

They can be heard as songs of love or of longing, songs of encouragement or of comfort, songs of struggle or of security But most of all, they are the songs of life, giving testimony to what has been, giving praise for all we're given, giving hope for all we strive for, giving voice to the great mystery that carries each of us in and out of this world.

DAVID S. BLANCHARD

Listen to your father who begot you,
    and do not despise your mother when she is old.
Buy truth, and do not sell it;
    buy wisdom, instruction, and understanding.
The father of the righteous will greatly rejoice;
    he who begets a wise son will be glad in him.
Let your father and mother be glad;
    let her who bore you rejoice.

PROVERBS 23:22–25

Nothing is more important to our shared future than the well-being of children. For children are at our core—not only as vulnerable beings in need of love and care but as a moral touchstone amidst the complexity and contentiousness of modern life. Just as it takes a village to raise a child, it takes children to raise up a village to become all it should be. The village we build with them in mind will be a better place for us all.

HILLARY CLINTON

I think that God's love, God's acceptance, and God's grace come to us long before *we* choose to acknowledge them. If baptism is a receipt of grace, of God's blessing, I don't think we need to earn it by our own affirmations and choices. Can I say it this way: God loves us even before we love God?

THOMAS D. WINTLE

The general purpose of the dedication is always the same: to bless. We don't bless to make the child sacred but to express as parents and as a community our recognition of and devotion to the child's innate sacredness. We do not so much ask the divine to care as invoke the divine within the child. We commit ourselves to nurture this divinity.

We also bless life at the dedication by praising and glorifying and giving thanks to life, which gives us this sacred trust of a child. A final blessing commits us to protect the child from harm and to love and guide this child toward a life of goodness and happiness.

LOUIS V. SCHWEBIUS

Let us bless this child, joining in an act of love and beauty to bless her with the elements of our common creation and with the glory of her distinct and beautiful names.

With earth, which is as strong as your given frame, my child, we bless you. Take care of yourself as a body. Be good to yourself—for you are a good gift to this world.

With air, which moves and changes even as your given passions, my child, we bless you. You will know contentment and discontent, joy and sorrow, anger and deep love in your life. Feel your feelings, my child, for they are good gifts.

With fire, which is as illuminating as your given intellect, my child, we bless you. Think things through, and reason and question carefully, for the light that shines in your mind is a good gift.

With water, which is as clear as your spirit my child, we bless you. Enlarge in conscience and grow a deep and rich spiritual life, for spirit too, is a good gift, a welcome that quickens your heart and strengthens the character.

MARK BELLETINI

My child, eat honey, for it is good, and the drippings of the honeycomb are sweet to your taste. Know that wisdom is such to your soul; if you find it, you will find a future, and your hope will not be cut off.

PROVERBS 24:13–14

A Candle Lighting

Out of a primal darkness
    this child has come.
Into a world of light—
    herself a new light.

We light a candle
    to signify her coming
        and her being—
Light into Light.

Her solitary flame is yet a continuity,
sparked by paired and branching flames.

Look at the flame.
See many flames diverging/converging.

Light into Light into Light.

EDWARD SEARL

Of all the needs (there are none imaginary) a lonely child has, the one that must be satisfied, if there is going to be hope and a hope of wholeness, is the unshaken need for an unshakable God.

MAYA ANGELOU

A Wish for Children

We wish for you a storm or two that you may enjoy the calm. We wish for you tranquility in time of trial. We wish you a cool breeze on a warm day, and pale white clouds that you may better appreciate the blueness of the sky. We wish you darkness that you may see the stars.

We wish you anticipation of high adventure, and we wish you the courage to avoid battle. We wish you a sense of wonder—and poetry—and music. We wish you companionship that you may appreciate solitude.

We wish you a friend who will understand you, and understanding so that you may have a friend. We wish you may become all that you wish to be, and more than you hope that you can be.

We wish you a flower to smell, a hand to touch, a voice to cheer, a heart to gladden. And we wish you people to love, as we love you.

BOB KAUFMANN

I will speak of six wishes I have for all of our children, and of course, for all of us.

I hope that our children can learn to differentiate between opinion, prejudice, wishing, fantasizing, blowing off steam, and honoring the truth. I hope they will be able to know those occasions when they must value the truth more highly than anything else.

I hope that our children and grandchildren learn to live with some comfort in a world where judgments and even rejection happen to all of us. I hope they will be willing to be challenged and able to discern between judgments that carry the seeds of truth and those that teach nothing but the resilience to move beyond them.

I hope that all of our children will take responsibility for their inner lives, that they will find some way to prevent their hurts—past, present, or future—from defining who they are.

And I hope that our children will discover that they are incomplete by themselves, that maturity will bring them an understanding of that part of themselves that is encouraged by relationship with others. I hope our children find a goal for their lives that is greater than their own self-interest or values that are worthy of their firmest commitment. May we leave our children with integrity that will never be sacrificed on the altar of convenience.

My final wish for our children, our grandchildren, and ourselves is that they and we will not stop hoping for a better world or working to make that hope a reality.

JOHN H. NICHOLS

A Blessing for Mary Grace

Welcome, dearest child.
Welcome to your two families, rich heritages converging in you.
    There never has been, there never will be anyone like you.
You are unique!
Welcome to this world—so finely formed and fragile yet amazingly
    tenacious and abundant. It is shot through with so much beauty.
    Immerse yourself in the beauty. Live in harmony with your world.

Freely and gladly accept the bounty it offers.

Welcome to the marvelous era in which you were born. It promises
wondrous possibilities. You have before you unimaginable fron-
tiers, great discoveries, and new meanings.

Seize your days!

Welcome to your age on this earth. May you know a restless yearning
to be alive, to know, to reflect, and to make meaning. Always be
mindful of your place in an awesome universe. It is more than
your home. It is in you, even as you are in it.

It is your destiny and destination.

Welcome to the greatest journey in the universe, your journey lived
through the ongoing gift and graces of your being.

Be hopeful and joyful throughout your days.

In your newness the world is new too. Your mother and father, who
brought you into being in love, are so glad and grateful for you.
We rejoice with them. We promise to join them in loving nurture—that you may be fulfilled, even as your fulfillment fulfills
us too.

On this day of you birth and forevermore, we give you our love.

EDWARD SEARL

The Child's Name Is All Children

There is only one child in the world
and the child's name is All Children.

CARL SANDBURG

For nothing is fixed, forever and forever and forever, it is not fixed;
the earth is always shifting, the light is always changing, the sea does
not cease to grind down rock. Generations do not cease to be born,
and we are responsible to them because we are the only witnesses
they have.

The sea rises, the light fails, lovers cling to each other, and children cling to us. The moment we cease to hold each other, the
moment we break faith with one another, the sea engulfs us and the
light goes out.

JAMES BALDWIN

Like the leaves in their generations, such is the race of men.
For the wind casts the leaves from their branches to earthward, and
again
Others the budding greenwood each springtide brings to birth,
So do man's generations spring up and fade from earth.

HOMER

Before I came I was in the birdsong
announcing dawn,
in globes of dew
on needles of the spruce
dropping onto fallow fields.

I could hear gulls
spread sound over the sea,
colored blue by dawn light,
and feel swelling water
bounce off the ocean floor.

There in shafts of light
the bones of my ancestors
began to drum an echo,
and to that beat
stone pounded stone upon the shore.

Out of the rock came life,
animals ground seeds;
I inhaled life
in the first breath
that blew through a reed.

JACQUELINE BEAUREGARD

Baby Mine

Baby mine, over the trees;
    Baby mine, over the flowers;
Baby mine, over the sunshine;
    Baby mine, over the showers;

Baby mine, over the land;
    Baby mine, over the water.
Oh, when had a mother before
    Such a sweet—such a sweet, little daughter!

KATE GREENAWAY

My baby has a mottled fist,
My baby has a neck in creases;
My baby kisses and is kissed,
For he's the very thing for kisses.

CHRISTINA ROSSETTI

Baby Face

White moon comes in on a baby face.
The shafts across her bed are flimmering.

Out on the land White Moon shines,
Shines and glimmers against gnarled shadows,
All silver to slow twisted shadows
Falling across the long road that runs from the house.

Keep a little of your beauty
And some of your flimmering silver
For her by the window to-night
Where you come in, White Moon.

CARL SANDBURG

Baby

Baby in her slumber smiling,
Doth a captive take:
Whispers Love, "From dreams beguiling
May she never wake!"

When the lids, like mist retreating,
Flee the azure deep,
Wakes a newborn Joy, repeating,
"May she never sleep!"

Arrival of Hope

On winter's dawn she has come,
    rising in our hearts,
    spreading warmth
        on our coldest fears.

Who is she?
    An epiphany?
    A gift of time claimed from chaos?
    A mystery dissolved into tiny features?
    A face, feet, fingers?

We gaze into her eyes,
    and we see
    years of joy and sorrow.

We listen to her heart,
    and we hear the rhythm
    that connects us.
We touch her softness with our souls.
Steadily, this daughter of grace reveals us.
Firmly, the bud is set for spring.

STEPHEN SHICK

Dream on, for dreams are sweet:
    Do not awaken!
Dream on, and at thy feet
    Pomegranates shall be shaken.

Who likeneth the youth
    Of life to morning?
'Tis like the night in truth,
    Rose-coloured dreams adorning.

The wind is soft above,
    The shadows umber.
(There is a dream called Love.)
    Take thou the fullest slumber!

PAUL LAURENCE DUNBAR

A baby is God's opinion that the world should go on.

CARL SANDBURG

Hush! my dear, lie still and slumber,
    Holy angels guard thy bed!
Heavenly blessings without number
    Gently falling on thy head.

Sleep, my babe; thy food and raiment,
    House and home, thy friends provide;
All without thy care or payment:
    All thy wants are well supplied.

ISAAC WATTS

Lie a-bed,
Sleepy head,
Shut up eyes, bo-peep;
Till daybreak
Never wake:—
Baby, sleep.

CHRISTINA ROSSETTI

Sweet and Low

Sweet and Low, sweet and low
    Wind of the western sea,
Low, low, breathe and blow,
    Wind of the western sea!
Over the rolling waters go,
Come from the dying moon, and blow,
    Blow him again to me;
While my little one, while my pretty one sleeps.—

Sleep and rest, sleep and rest,
    Father will come to thee soon;
Rest, rest, on mother's breast,
    Father will come to thee soon;
Father will come to his babe in the next,
Silver sails all out of the west
    Under the silver moon;
Sleep, my little one, sleep, my pretty one, sleep.

ALFRED LORD TENNYSON

Gold and Love for Dearie

Out on the mountain over the town,
    All night long, all night long,
The trolls go up and the trolls go down,
    Bearing their packs and crooning a song;
And this is the song the hill-folk croon,
As they trudge in the light of the misty moon,—
This is ever their dolorous tune:
"Gold, gold! ever more gold,—
       Bright red gold for dearie!"

Deep in the hill the yeoman delves
    All night long, all night long;
None but the peering, furtive elves
    See his toil and hear his song;
Merrily ever the cavern rings
As merrily ever his pick he swings,
And merrily ever this song he sings:
"Gold, gold! ever more gold,—
       Bright red gold for dearie!"

Mother is rocking thy lowly bed
    All night long, all night long,
Happy to smooth thy curly head
    And to hold thy hand and to sing her song;

'T is not of the hill-folk, dwarfed and old,
Nor the song of the yeoman, stanch and bold,
And the burden it beareth is not of gold;
But it's "Love, love!—nothing but love,—
Mother's love for dearie!"

EUGENE FIELD

Ho! Soft art thou,
    Smooth thou, soft thou!
Well I love thee,
    Smooth thou, soft thou!
Well I love thee,
    Smooth thou, soft thou!
Under the plaid,
    Smooth thou, soft thou!
Well I love thee,
    Smooth thou, soft thou!
In the morning
    Soft-white, red-bright.
Well I love thee,
    Smooth thou, soft thou!
I, to companion thee,
    I to lull thee.

I to fill thee
    With the fondnesses,
I, to fill thee
    From the breast of thy mother.
Soft thou! Soft thou!
    Soft my little love!
Soft as silk to thee
    The heart of thy mother!

SCOTTISH LULLABY

Lullaby of the Iroquois

Little brown baby-bird, lapped in your nest,
Wrapped in your nest,
Strapped in your nest,
Your straight little cradle-board rocks you to rest;
Its hands are your nest;
Its bands are your nest;
It swings from the down-bending branch of the oak;
You watch the camp flame, and the curling grey smoke;
But, oh, for your pretty black eyes sleep is best,—
Little brown baby of mine, go to rest.
Little brown baby-bird swinging to sleep,

Winging to sleep,
Singing to sleep,
Your wonder-black eyes that so wide open keep,
Shielding their sleep,
Unyielding to sleep,
The heron is homing, the plover is still,
The night-owl calls from his haunt on the hill,
Afar the fox barks, afar the stars peep,—
Little brown baby of mine, go to sleep.

EMILY PAULINE JOHNSON (TEKAHIONWAKE)

Cradle Song

What does little birdie say
In her nest at peep of day?
Let me fly, says little birdie,
Mother, let me fly away.
Birdie, rest a little longer,
Till thy little wings are stronger.
So she rests a little longer,
Then she flies away.

What does little baby say,
In her bed at peep of day?
Baby says, like little birdie,
Let me rise and fly away.
Baby, sleep a little longer,
Till thy little limbs are stronger.
If she sleeps a little longer,
Baby too shall fly away.

ALFRED LORD TENNYSON

Lullaby

Lullaby, and good night,
With pink roses bedight,
With lilies o'erspread,
Is my baby's sweet head.
Lay you down now, and rest,
May your slumber be blessed!
Lay you down now, and rest,
May thy slumber be blessed!

Lullaby, and good night,
You're your mother's delight,
Shining angels beside

My darling abide.
Soft and warm is your bed,
Close your eyes and rest your head.
Soft and warm is your bed,
Close your eyes and rest your head.

Sleepyhead, close your eyes.
Mother's right here beside you.
I'll protect you from harm,
You will wake in my arms.
Guardian angels are near,
So sleep on, with no fear.
Guardian angels are near,
So sleep on, with no fear.

Lullaby, and sleep tight.
Hush! My darling is sleeping,
On his sheets white as cream,
With his head full of dreams.
When the sky's bright with dawn,
He will wake in the morning.
When noontide warms the world,
He will frolic in the sun.

JOHANN BRAHMS

Love me,—I love you,
Love me, my baby;
Sing it high, sing it low,
Sing it as may be.

Mother's arms under you,
Her eyes above you;
Sing it high, sing it low,
Love me—I love you.

CHRISTINA ROSSETTI

Lullaby, oh, lullaby!
Flowers are closed and lambs are sleeping;
    Lullaby, oh, lullaby!
Stars are up, the moon is peeping;
    Lullaby, oh, lullaby!
While the birds are silence keeping,
    (Lullaby, oh, lullaby!)
Sleep, my baby, fall a-sleeping,
    Lullaby, oh, lullaby!

CHRISTINA ROSSETTI

Parent's Affirmation

I love you.
I am your parent; you are my child.
There is no more sacred bond.
In all the days and years to come,
I promise you my loving care,
providing you both roots and wings,
that you may feel safe, that you may one day fly.
I am glad you have entered my life.
I love you.

LINDSAY BATES

First Footsteps

A little way, more soft and sweet
Than fields aflower with May,
A babe's feet, venturing, scarce complete
A little way.

Eyes full of dawning day
Look up for mother's eyes to meet,
Too blithe for song to say.

Glad as the golden spring to greet
Its first live leaflet's play,
Love, laughing, leads the little feet
A little way.

ALGERNON CHARLES SWINBURNE

Mother's Treasures

Two little children sit by my side,
I call them Lily and Daffodil;
I gaze on them with a mother's pride,
One is Edna, the other is Will.

Both have eyes of starry light,
And laughing lips o'er teeth of pearl.
I would not change for a diadem
My noble boy and darling girl.

To-night my heart o'erflows with joy;
I hold them as a sacred trust;
I fain would hide them in my heart,
Safe from tarnish of moth and rust.

What should I ask for my dear boy?
The richest gifts of wealth or fame?
What for my girl? A loving heart
And a fair and a spotless name?

What for my boy? That he should stand
A pillar of strength to the state?
What for my girl? That she should be
The friend of the poor and desolate?

I do not ask they shall never tread
With weary feet the paths of pain.
I ask that in the darkest hour
They may faithful and true remain.

I only ask their lives may be
Pure as gems in the gates of pearl,
Lives to brighten and bless the world-
This I ask for my boy and girl.

FRANCES ELLEN WATKINS HARPER

My Sons

Sometimes my sons are Children of the Sun,
intense and radiant,
excited and streaming with energy.

Sometimes my sons are Children of the Stars,
steady and ever-present,
independent and limitless.

Sometimes my sons are Children of the Moon,
cool and distant,
not avoiding but not reaching out.

Sometimes my sons are Children of Venus,
affectionate and loving,
close and considerate.

Sometimes my sons are Children of Mars,
defiant and challenging,
determined and strong-willed.

Sometimes my sons are Children of Jupiter,
deep and mysterious,
dramatic and powerful.

Sometimes my sons are Children of Saturn,
beautiful and creative,
delicate and fragile.

Sometimes my sons are Children of the Comet,
wandering,
curious, investigating.

Sometimes my sons are Children of the Meteor,
suddenly chaotic,
violent and majestic.

My sons are Children of the Earth,
solid and grounded,
resilient and self-confident,
Children of Creation.

KIT LUEDER

First Day of School

No matter what they tell you,
Let it be about joy
Let it be about the sacred
Self surviving—no, thriving—
Shining its way to the knowledge within.
Let it be about blooming,
The unfolding of the universe through you,
Because the story of you begins
Fifteen billion years ago
With that first flash of being.

At four, you reached out your hand
Into the dark night and pulled
Back in wonder, a firefly blinking
From your finger. Keep that magic,
That both you and the firefly are one,
Everything connected,
Everything possible,
Made of stardust and moonshine as
We all are.
Let it always be
About
Your shining.

NITA PENFOLD

What is the world, if not a playground for children?
What is living for, its labors, if not for the season of
   birth and becoming?
Children move from the family into their lives, having
   determined who they are, having measured the
   world, having received a face and a name.
Civilization is the nurture of the child, its supportive
   world, or it is nothing.

KENNETH PATTON

I Do Not Have Children

I do not have a child, but I know that this is neither a reason nor an excuse for new generations to go without my experience, my vision, or my care. I do not have to have my own children to love what children bring to this world, to help them, hold them, inspire them, and make them capable of living on the level of their dreams.

I can teach. As long as I have beliefs infused with truth and love and a place to act out my beliefs, I can make a difference. And in so doing, I have many children. And I have a legacy. I can change the world.

GREG WARD

It is not possible for civilization to flow backward while there is youth in the world.

HELEN KELLER

Nothing that is worth doing is completed in our lifetime; therefore, we must be saved by hope. . . . Nothing we do, however virtuous, can be accomplished alone; therefore, we are saved by love.

REINHOLD NIEBUHR

The wolf shall live with the lamb,
the leopard shall lie down with the kid,
the calf and the lion and the fatling together,
and a little child shall lead them.

ISAIAH 11:6

From birth to death we shine like stars and then explode, and our lives are recapitulations of that original creating.

VICTORIA SAFFORD

For each child that's born, a morning star rises and sings to the
    universe who we are.
We are our grandmother's prayers and
We are our grandfather's dreamings,
We are the breath of our ancestors,
We are the spirit of God.
We are mothers of courage and fathers of time,
We are daughters of dust and the sons of great visions,
We're sisters of mercy and brothers of love,
We are lovers of life and the builders of nations,
We're seekers of truth and keepers of faith,
We are makers of peace and the wisdom of ages.

YSAYE M. BARNWELL

You are as precious as the birds or the tulips or the tree whose
crenelated bark protects the insects who seek its shelter. You are an
amazing, complex being, with poetry in your arteries, and charity
layered beneath your skin.

ELIZABETH TARBOX

Index of First Lines

Credits

Selections appear on page numbers in bold.

ANDREWS   *A Passion for this Earth: Exploring a New Partnership of Man, Woman, and Nature* (**27**) by Valerie Andrews, 1992.

ANGELOU   *I Know Why the Caged Bird Sings* (**119**) by Maya Angelou, 1969.

ANONYMOUS   *Child Naming/Parent Dedication Booklet* (**89**), First Unitarian Universalist Congregation of Ottawa, Ontario, date unknown.

BACON   "Of Marriage and Single Life" (**63**) and "Of Parents and Children" (**72**), in *Essays, Civil and Moral* by Francis Bacon, 1601.

BALDWIN   *Nothing Personal* (**125**) by James Baldwin, 1964.

BARNWELL   "We Are" (**148**) by Ysaye M. Barnwell, © 1991 Barnwell's Notes Publishing. Used with permission of Ysaye M. Barnwell.

BATES   "Parent's Affirmation" (**140**). Used with permission of Lindsay Bates (**14, 73, 74, 140**).

BEAUREGARD   "From Song to Echo" (**126**), in *How We Are Called*, edited by Mary Benard and Kirstie Anderson, 2003. Used with permission of Jacqueline Beauregard.

BELLETINI   Used with permission of Mark Belletini. (**117**)

BLAKE   "Spring" (**44**), "A Cradle Song" (**53**), and "On Another's Sorrow" (**71**), in *Songs of Innocence* by William Blake, 1789.

BLANCHARD   "Listening for Our Song" (**114**), in *A Temporary State of Grace* by David S. Blanchard, 1997. Used with permission of the author.

BODNAR   Used with permission of Katherine Searl Bodnar. (**36**)

BOLZ   "Brit Kedusha" (**34**), in *Jewish Currents*, 1989. Used with permission of Jody Bolz.

BOOK OF COMMON PRAYER   "Prayers for the Natural Order" (**111**), in *Book of Common Prayer.*

BOULTON   "All Through the Night" (**112**) by Harold Boulton, in *Folk Songs of England, Ireland, Scotland and Wales*, edited by William Cole, 1961.

BRAHMS   *Lullaby* (**137**), by Johann Brahms, source unknown.

BYRON   *Cain* (**12**, **56**) by George Gordon Lord Byron, 1821.

CABLE   "The New Arrival" (**40**) by George Washington Cable, in *An American Anthology: 1787–1900*, edited by Edmund Clarence Stedman, 1900.

CARROLL   Inscription in *The Hunting of the Snark* (**4**) by Lewis Carroll, 1872.

CARSON   *The Sense of Wonder* (**3**, **100**) by Rachel Carson, 1956.

CARTER   *Where Main Street Meets the River* (**59**) by Hodding Carter, 1953.

CHANNING   "The Great End in Religious Instruction" (**95**) by William Ellery Channing, in *Singing the Living Tradition*, 1993.

CHILD   *Philothea* (**99**) by Lydia Maria Child, 1836.

CLIFTON   "won't you celebrate with me" (**67**), in *The Book of Light*, copyright © 1993 by Lucille Clifton. Used with permission of Copper Canyon Press, P.O. Box 271, Port Townsend, WA 98368-0271.

CLINTON   Floor speech at Democratic National Convention (**86**) by Hillary Rodham Clinton, 1996. *It Takes a Village* (**116**) by Hillary Rodham Clinton, 1996.

COLEMAN   "Black Baby" (**43**) by Anita Scott Coleman, in *Shadowed Dreams: Women's Poetry of the Harlem Renaissance*, edited by Maureen Honey, 1989.

COLERIDGE   "The Child" (**87**) by Sara Coleridge, in *The Oxford Book of English Verse: 1250–1900*, edited by Arthur Quiller-Couch, 1900.

CUMMINS   *Rejoice Together: Prayers, Meditations and Other Readings for Family, Individual and Small Group Worship* (**71**), collected by Helen R. Pickett, 1995. Used with permission of John Cummins.

DAVID   Used with permission of Anthony David (**12**, **107**).

DAVIES   *What's Bred in the Bone* (**66**) by Robertson Davies, 1985.

DICKENS   *The Old Curiosity Shop* (**64**) by Charles Dickens, 1840.

DOWGIERT   "Let the Children Come" (**8**, **74**). Used with permission of Diane Dowgiert.

DUNBAR   "Dreams" (**130**), in *The Complete Poems of Paul Laurence Dunbar*, edited by William Dean Howells, 1993.

EDELMAN   *The Measure of Our Success* (**85**) by Marion Wright Edelman, 1992.

EDWARDS "A Child's Prayer" (**114**), in *Good Words* by Matilda B. B. Edwards, 1873.

ELLIS "The Spirituality of Children" (**94**). Used with permission of Kathleen Ellis.

EMERSON "Nominalist and Realist" (**5**) and "Nature" (**25**, **28**), in *Essays: Second Series* by Ralph Waldo Emerson, 1844. "The Over-Soul" (**82**), in *Essays: First Series* by Ralph Waldo Emerson, 1841.

FAHS "For So the Children Come" (**41**) and "It Matters What We Believe" (**96**) by Sophia Lyon Fahs, in *Singing the Living Tradition*, 1993.

FIELD "The Divine Lullaby" (**105**), in *John Smith, U. S. A.* by Eugene Field, 1905. "Gold and Love for Dearie" (**133**), in *Poems of Childhood* by Eugene Field, 1904.

FINKELSTEIN Used with permission of Roberta Finkelstein (**81**).

FOLLEN "On Hearing of the Sadness of the Slave-Children from the Fear of Being Sold" (**69**) by Eliza Lee Cabot Follen, in *Standing Before Us: Unitarian Universalist Women and Social Reform, 1776–1936*, edited by Dorothy May Emerson, 1999.

FULGHUM *All I Really Need to Know I Learned in Kindergarten* (**26**) by Robert Fulghum, 1986.

GIBRAN "On Children" (**61**), in *The Prophet* by Kahlil Gibran, 1923.

GRAVES "Babylon" (**16**), in *Fairies and Fusiliers* by Robert Graves, 1918.

GREENAWAY "Baby Mine" (**127**), in *Marigold Garden* by Kate Greenaway, 1885.

GUEST   "Home and the Baby" (**50**), in *Just Folks* by Edgar Albert Guest, 1917.

HARPER   "Thank God for Little Children" (**18**) and "Mother's Treasures" (**141**), in *Poems* by Frances Ellen Watkins Harper, 1900.

HASIDIC PROVERB   Source unknown (**104**).

HIGGINSON   "A Shadow" (**36**), in *Old Port Days* by Thomas Wentworth Higginson, 1873.

HOERTDOERFER   "Kasserian Ingera: How Are the Children?" (**92**). Used with permission of Patricia Hoertdoerfer.

HOLLAND   "Babyhood" (**45**) by Josiah Gilbert Holland, in *An American Anthology 1787–1900*, edited by Edmund Clarence Stedman, 1900. "Where Shall the Baby's Dimple Be?" (**55**), 1883.

HOMER   The *Iliad* (**125**) by Homer, translated by F. L. Lucas, 1950.

HUBBELL   "Choose Peace" (**109**). Used with permission of Phyllis L. Hubbell.

HUXLEY   "Vulgarity in Literature" (**26**), in *Music at Night* by Aldous Huxley, 1931.

INGERSOLL   "Liberty of Man, Woman and Child" (**26**), in *The Lectures of Col. R. G. Ingersoll* by Robert Green Ingersoll, 1898.

ISAIAH   Isaiah 11:6, New Revised Standard Version (**147**).

JACK   "Kids Are Great!" (**15**, **78**). Used with permission of Cheryl Jack.

JOHNSON   Selection by Samuel Johnson (**47**), in *Rambler*, August 1751.

JOHNSON   "Lullaby of the Iroquois" (**135**), in *Canadian Born* by Emily Pauline Johnson (Tekahionwake), 1903.

JONG   "The Birth of the Water Baby" (**33**), copyright Erica Mann Jong © 1983. All rights reserved. Used with permission of Erica Mann Jong.

JORDAN   *Some of Us Did Not Die* (**28**) by June Jordan, 2002.

KAUFMANN   "A Wish for Children" (**119**) by Bob Kaufmann, in *Rejoice Together*, collected by Helen R. Pickett, 1995.

KELLER   *Midstream* (**147**) by Helen Keller, 1930.

KING   *The Real Miracle* (**4**) by Donald B. King, date unknown.

KING   "Standing in the Dark" (**98**), in *How We Are Called*, edited by Mary Benard and Kirstie Anderson, 2003. Used with permission of Pat King.

LAO TZU   *Tao Te Ching* (**63**, **83**) by Lao Tzu, translated by J. H. McDonald, 1996.

LONGFELLOW   "Children" (**16**) by Henry Wadsworth Longfellow, in *English Poetry III: From Tennyson to Whitman*, edited by Charles W. Eliot, 1909. "My Lost Youth" (**28**), "The Children's Hour" (**64**), and "The Fiftieth Birthday of Agassiz" (**105**), in *Birds of Passage* by Henry Wadsworth Longfellow, 1858.

LUEDER   "My Sons" (**143**), in *For All That Is Our Life*, edited by Helen and Eugene Pickett, 2005. Used with permission of Kit Lueder.

MANDELA   Interview with Nelson Mandela (**85**) at www.timeforkids.com.

MARK   Mark 10:13–16, New Revised Standard Version (**99**).

MASTERS   "Columbus Cheney" (**73**), in *Spoon River Anthology* by Edgar Lee Masters, 1916.

MCTIGUE   Used with permission of Kathleen McTigue (**33**, **75**, **77**).

MIKELSON   "The Spirit of Children" (**15**). Used with permission of Thomas Mikelson.

MORLEY   *Mince Pie* (**51**) by Christopher Morley, 1919.

NICHOLS   Used with permission of John H. Nichols (**120**).

NIEBUHR   *The Irony of American History* (**147**) by Reinhold Niebuhr, 1952.

NIEUWEJAAR   *The Gift of Faith: Tending the Spiritual Lives of Children* (**97**) by Jeanne Harrison Nieuwejaar, 2002.

NOONEY   Used with permission of Gregory L. Nooney (**80**).

NOUWEN   *Life of the Beloved: Spiritual Living in a Secular World* (**106**) by Henri Nouwen, 1992.

OMAHA PRAYER   Adaptation from Omaha prayer (**103**) in *The Path on the Rainbow*, edited by George W. Cronyn, 1918.

O'QUILL   "Childhood Imagination" (**76**). Used with permission of Jennifer O'Quill.

OWEN-TOWLE   Used with permission of Carolyn S. Owen-Towle (**93**).

OZICK   "The Shock of Teapots" (**100**), in *Metaphor and Memory* by Cynthia Ozick, 1989.

PATTON   *Man Is the Meaning* (**11**) by Kenneth Patton, 1956. "The Fullness of the Moment" (**12**) by Kenneth Patton, in *Services and Songs in Celebration of Life,* 1967. *This World My Home* (**14**) by Kenneth Patton, 1966. "The Family" (**146**), in *A Religion of Realities* by Kenneth Patton, 1977. Used with permission of Clarice E. Patton.

PENFOLD   "First Day of School" (**145**), in *For All That Is Our Life,* edited by Helen and Eugene Pickett, 2005. Used with permission of Nita Penfold.

PETTITT   Used with permission of June Pettitt (**113**).

PHILIPS   "To Charlotte Pulteney" (**46**) by Ambrose Philips, in *The Golden Treasury,* edited by Francis T. Palgrave, 1875.

PLATO   *The Republic* (**88**) by Plato, edited by G. R. F. Ferrari, translated by Tom Griffith, 2000.

PROVERBS   Proverbs 23:22–25 (**115**) and 24:13–14 (**118**), New Revised Standard Version.

READ-BROWN   Used with permission of Ken Read-Brown (**90**).

ROOSEVELT   *Tomorrow Is Now* (**59**) by Eleanor Roosevelt, 1963. *You Learn by Living* (**89**, **92**, **93**) by Eleanor Roosevelt, 1960.

ROSSETTI   *Sing-Song* (**38**, **54**, **127**, **131**, **139**) by Christina Rossetti, 1872.

SAFFORD   "God Is What Knows How to Grow" (**147**), in *Walking Toward Morning* by Victoria Safford, 2003. Used with permission of the author.

SAINT-ÉXUPÉRY   *The Little Prince* (**25**) by Antoine de Saint-Éxupéry, 1943. *The Wisdom of the Sands* (**89**) by Antoine de Saint-Éxupéry, 1950.

SANDBURG   "Poppies" (**38**) from "Poems Done on a Late Night Car, III, Home" (**38, 88**), in *Chicago Poems* by Carl Sandburg, 1916. "Prologue" (**125**), in *The Family of Man* by Carl Sandburg, 1955. "Baby Face" (**128**), in *Cornhuskers* by Carl Sandburg, 1918. *Remembrance Rock* (**131**) by Carl Sandburg, 1948.

SCHWEBIUS   Used with permission of Louis V. Schwebius. (**116**)

SCOTT   "Of a Foolish Father" (**99**) by Clinton Lee Scott, in *The Gift of Faith: Tending the Spiritual Lives of Children* by Jeanne Harrison Nieuwejaar, 2002.

SCOTTISH LULLABY   *Carmina Gadelica* (**134**), edited by Alexander Carmichael, 1900.

SEARL   "Find Out" (**51**). Used with permission of Eloise Volckmann Searl.

SEN   *Nava Samhita* (**112**) by Keshub Chandra Sen, 1881.

SHAKESPEARE   *The Merchant of Venice* (**72**) by William Shakespeare, c. 1596.

SHAW   "Treatise on Parents and Children" (**13**), in *Misalliance* by George Bernard Shaw, 1909.

SHICK   "Arrival of Hope" (**129**), in *Consider the Lilies* by Stephen Shick, 2004. Used with permission of the author.

SMALL   "Everything Possible" (**59**), words and music by Fred Small © 1983 Pine Barrens Music (BMI), recorded on *Everything Possible: Fred Small in Concert* (Flying Fish 70625), available at www.rounder.com.

SOMÉ   *Welcoming Spirit Home* (**23**) by Sobonfu Somé, 1999. *The Gift of Happiness* (**86**) by Sobonfu Somé, date unknown.

Southern   Used with permission of Vanessa Rush Southern. (**19**)

Stafford   *Learning to Live in this World* (**25**) by William Stafford, 1994.

Sternberg   Used with permission of Connie Sternberg (**110**).

Stone   Selection by Elizabeth Stone (**56**), quoted by Ellen Cantarow in *The Village Voice*, date unknown.

Strong   Adaptation from "A Rosary of Things Beautiful" by Harry Youlden (**108**). Used with permission of Elizabeth M. Strong.

Swinburne   "Comparisons" (**6**), "Babyhood" (**8**), "Étude Réaliste" (**48**), and "First Footsteps" (**140**), in *A Century of Roundels* by Algernon Charles Swinburne, 1883.

Tabb   "Baby" (**128**), in *Poems* by John Bannister Tabb, 1906.

Talmud   Selection from Talmud (**82**), in *The Wisdom of Israel* by Lewis Browne, 1945.

Tarbox   "Mother's Day" (**113**), in *Life Tides* by Elizabeth Tarbox, 1993. "Rebirth" (**148**), in *Evening Tide* by Elizabeth Tarbox, 1998. Used with permission of Sarah Tarbox.

Taylor   Used with permission of Alan Taylor (**79**).

Tennyson   "Sweet and Low" (**132**), in *The Princess* by Alfred Lord Tennyson, 1847. "Cradle Song" (**136**), source unknown, 1851.

Thompson   *Shelley* (**5**) by Francis Thompson, 1909.

Thoreau   *Walden* (**27**) by Henry David Thoreau, 1854.

TRAHERNE   "The Salutation" (**39**) by Thomas Traherne, source unknown.

TRUEBLOOD   "God Bless Babies" (**54**) by Roscoe Trueblood, in *I Was Alive and Glad*, 1971. Used with permission of First Parish Unitarian Universalist in Cohasset, Massachusetts.

UNITED NATIONS   Adaptation from "Declaration of the Rights of the Child" (**67**) by the General Assembly of the United Nations, 1959.

UNTERMEYER   "On the Birth of a Child" (**42**), in *Modern American Poetry*, edited by Louis Untermeyer, 1919.

WALLACE   "What Rules the World" (**83**), in *What Rules the World* by William Ross Wallace, 1865.

WARD   "I Do Not Have Children" (**146**), in *For All That Is Our Life*, edited by Helen and Eugene Pickett, 2005. Used with permission of Greg Ward.

WATTS   "A Cradle Hymn" (**131**) by Isaac Watts, in *The Oxford Book of English Verse: 1250–1900*, edited by Arthur Quiller-Couch, 1919.

WELLEMEYER   Used with permission of Mary Wellemeyer (**21**, **35**).

WHITMAN   "There was a Child went Forth" (**3**) by Walt Whitman, in *Leaves of Grass,* 1855.

WILLIAMS   Used with permission of Betsy Hill Williams (**85**).

WILLIAMSON   *A Return to Love* (**104**) by Marianne Williamson, 1992.

WINNER   "Dreams That Charm'd Me When a Child" (**24**) by Septimus Winner, 1855.

WINTLE   Used with permission of Thomas D. Wintle (**116**).

WORDSWORTH   "Ode on Intimations of Immortality" (**4, 23**), in *The Complete Poetical Works* by William Wordsworth, 1888.

WORLD RELIGIOUS LEADERS   Adaptation from "The World's Religions for the World's Children" by World Religious Leaders (**71**), 1990.

YORK   "Give Us the Child" (**22**), in *Into the Wilderness* by Sarah York, 1990. Used with permission of the author.